The Beauty of Okmulgee's Historic Architecture

Ready for an adventure?

Okmulgee is a city with a rich and varied history. Part of that history is found in the buildings constructed during its past. The photos in this book point to a time when it wasn't acceptable just to build utilitarian buildings, as good and strong as they were. No, a building had to have beauty built into its walls, windows, doorways, and roof lines. Those details are featured in these photos.

All of the cornices, colonnades, crestings, cupolas, lunettes, moldings, reliefs, spandrels and turrets in these photos are all right here in Okmulgee. Too often we walk by them without noticing that they are there.

This book is intended to be an adventure book. The structures are here – can you find them? Can you identify them? Take your book with you and give it a try!

Here is an example. The first photo below is of an architectural item for which you are searching. Alongside of that photo is a hint. Next, I have given you a larger photo of the building where it is found – but only for the first one. You will have to conduct a search for the rest of them. I hope you have a good time discovering Okmulgee's hidden treasures.

Try looking at the seat of city government.

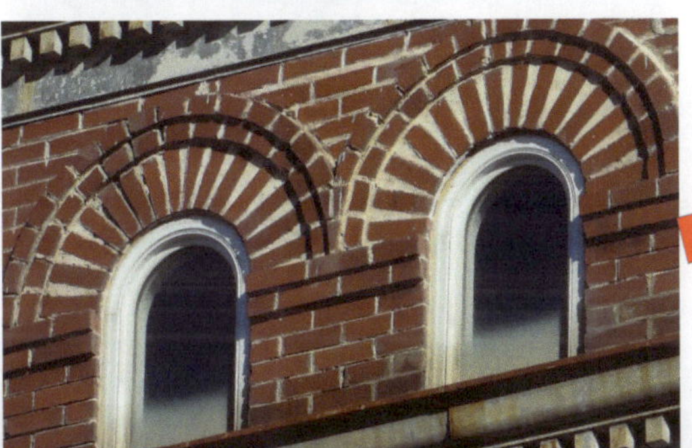

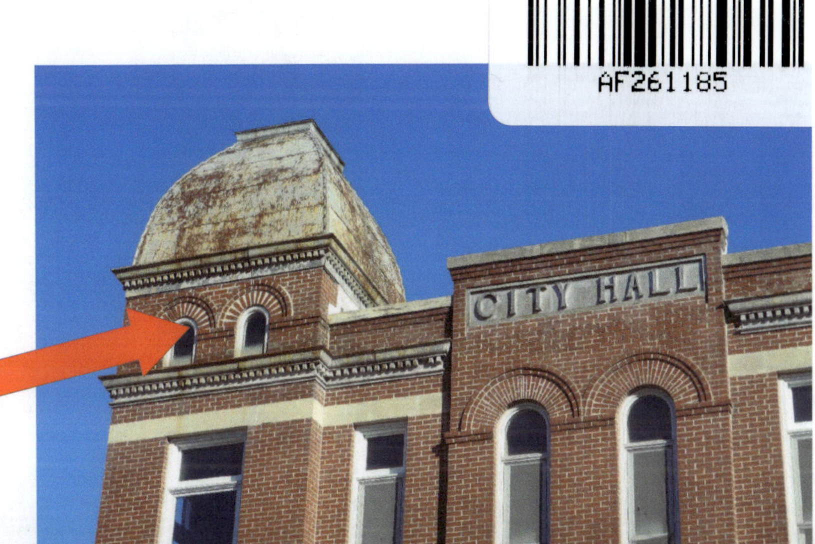

The first one
is out of the
downtown
area. It is
closer to
HWY 75. Try
looking on
Third Street.

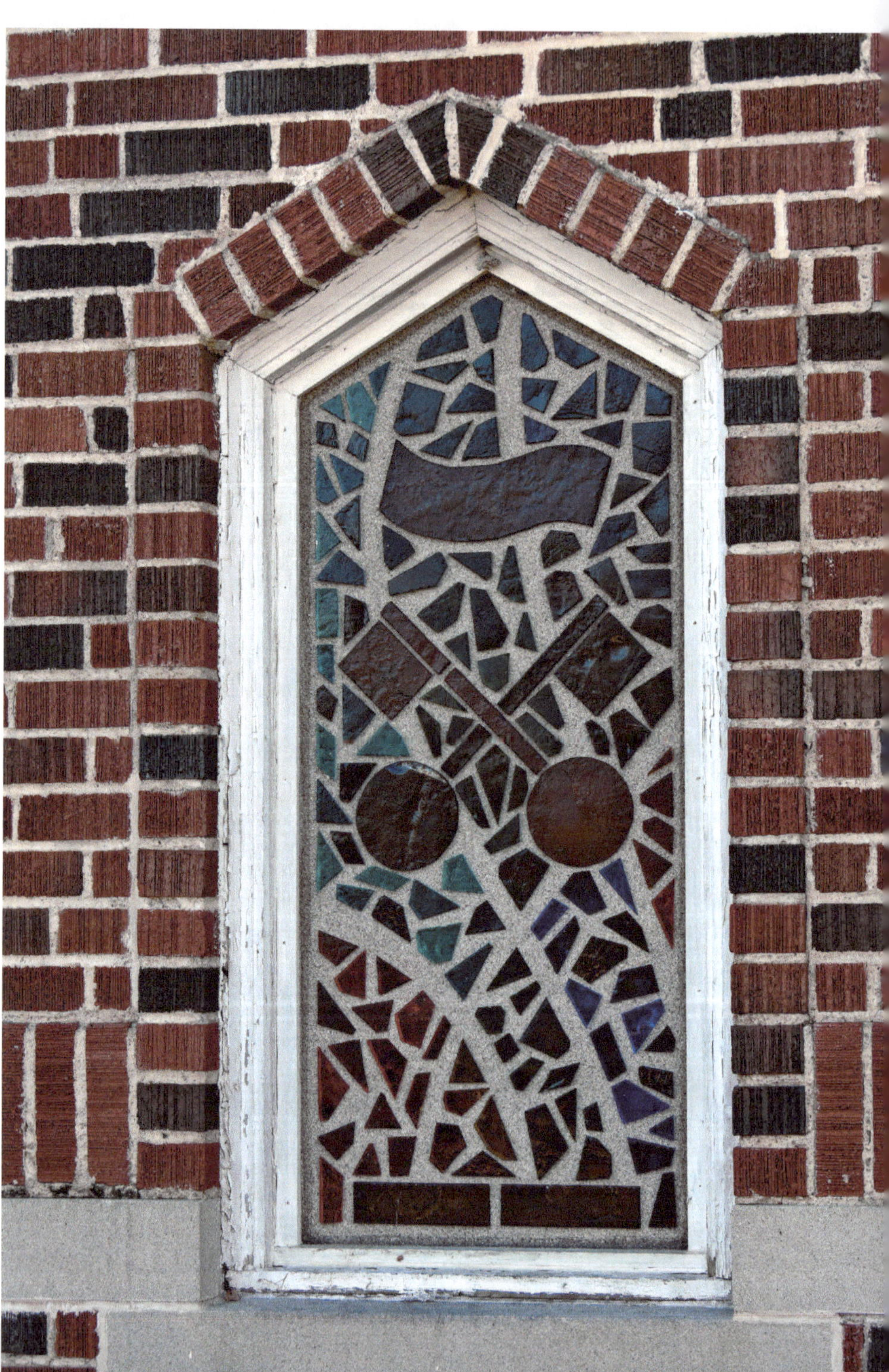

Don't try to do these in order; it would be better to keep looking at all of them as you go across town. This one is found on one of our oldest churches. Try looking south of the Methodist Church.

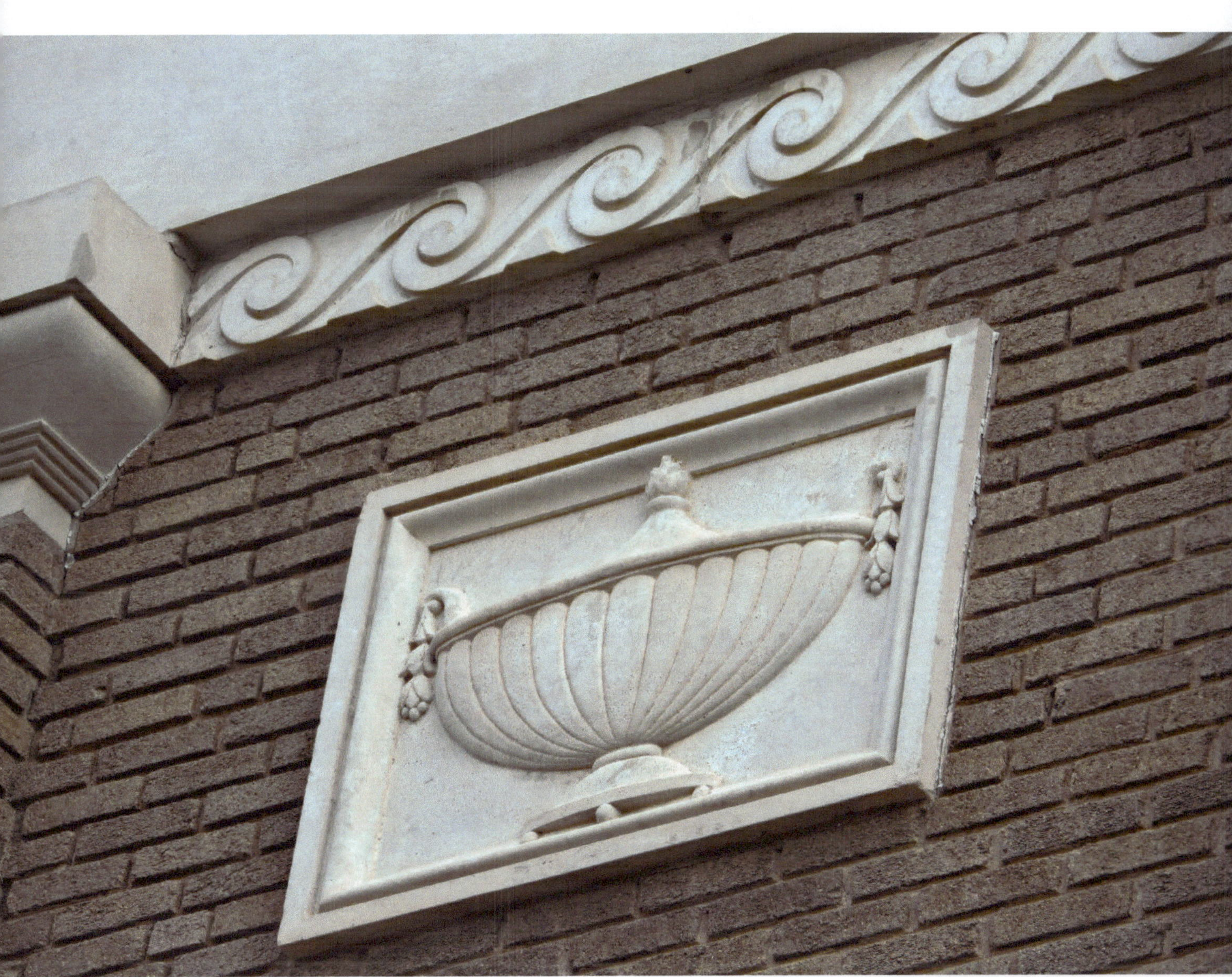

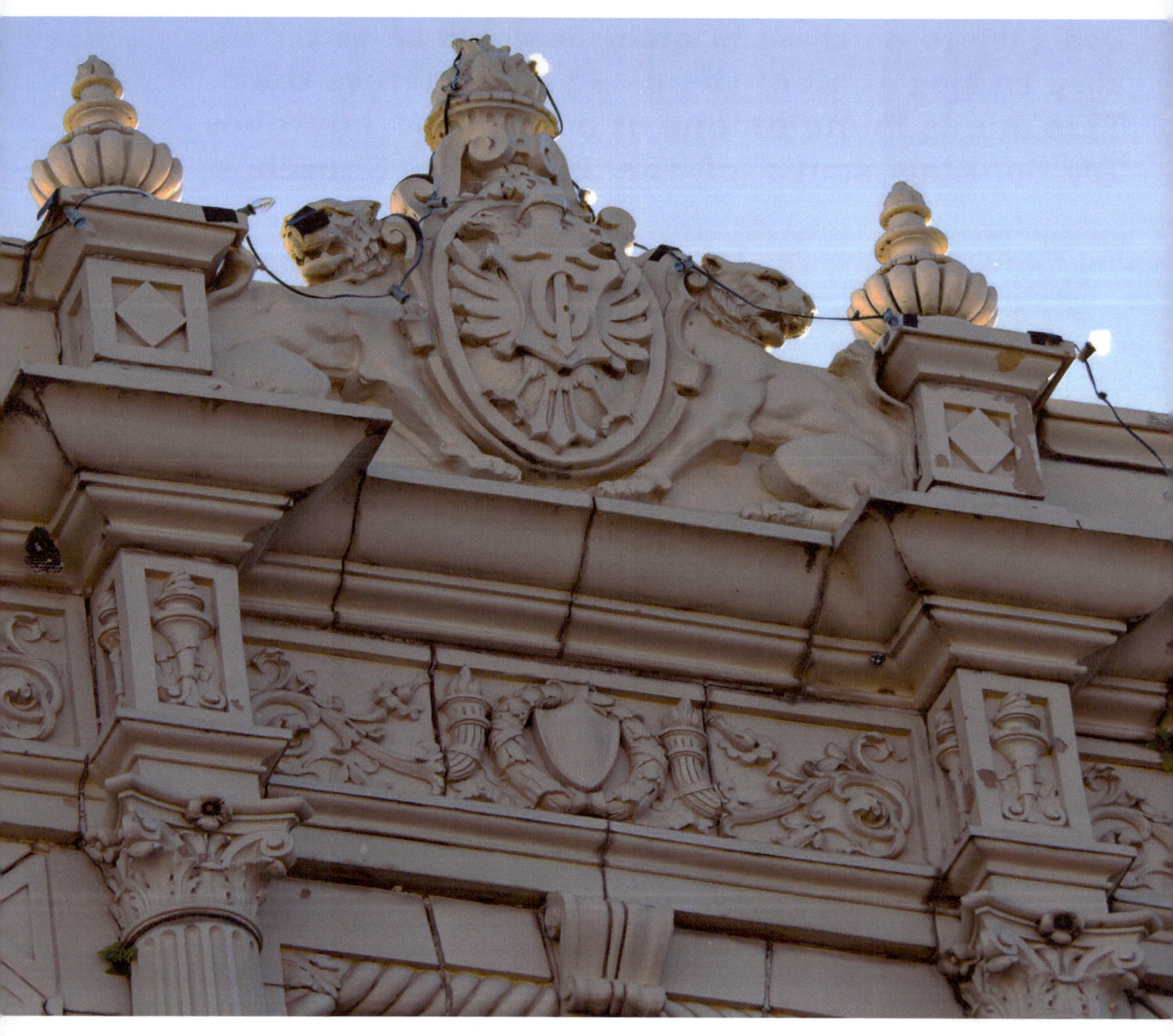

Some of the architecture is quite ornate. Look for this one where dances and shows are performed.

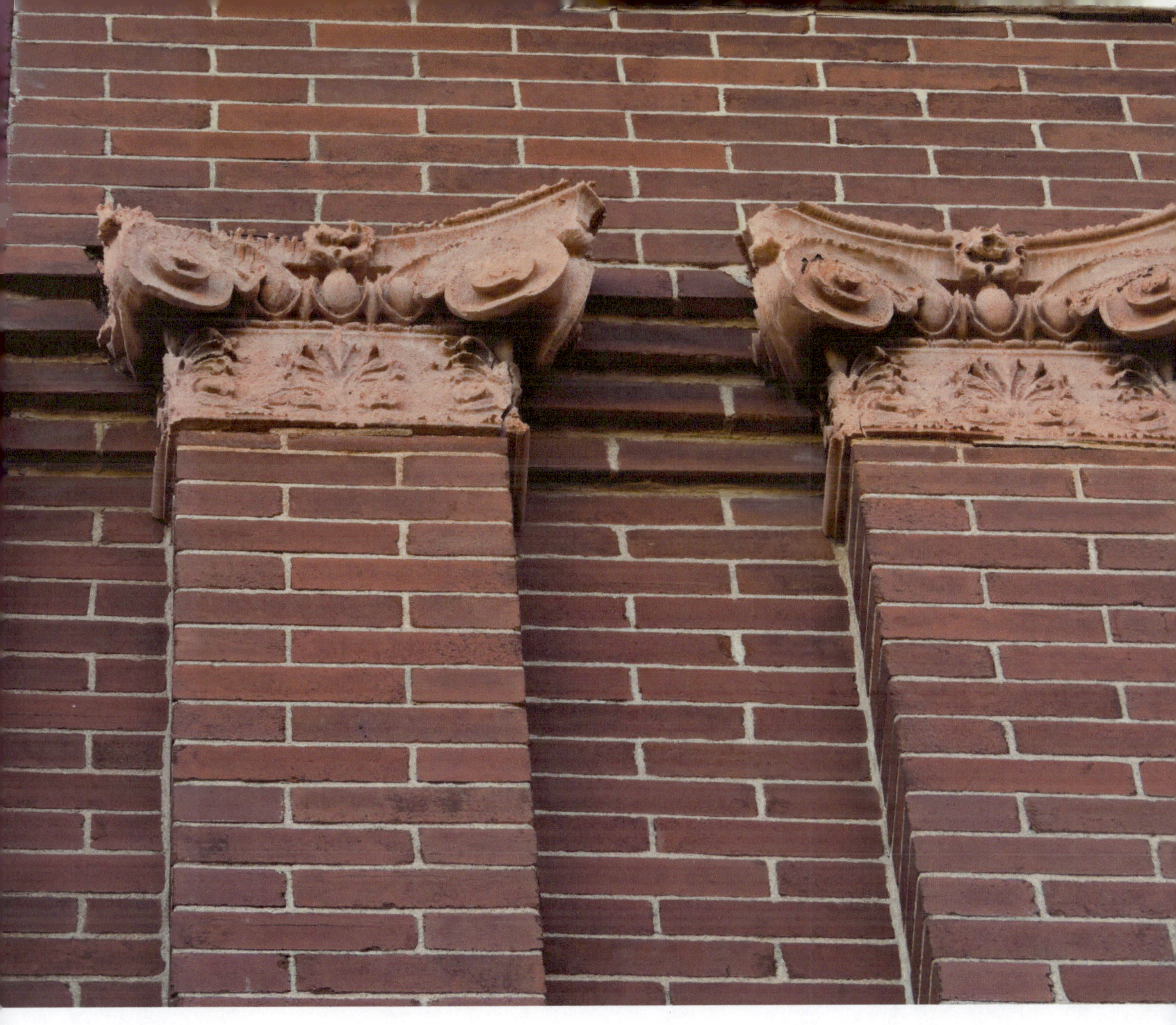

There are many architectural works along 6th Street. Narrow it down by looking for the Collin Building.

You can find this one where they store legal documents and where you go to get a marriage license.

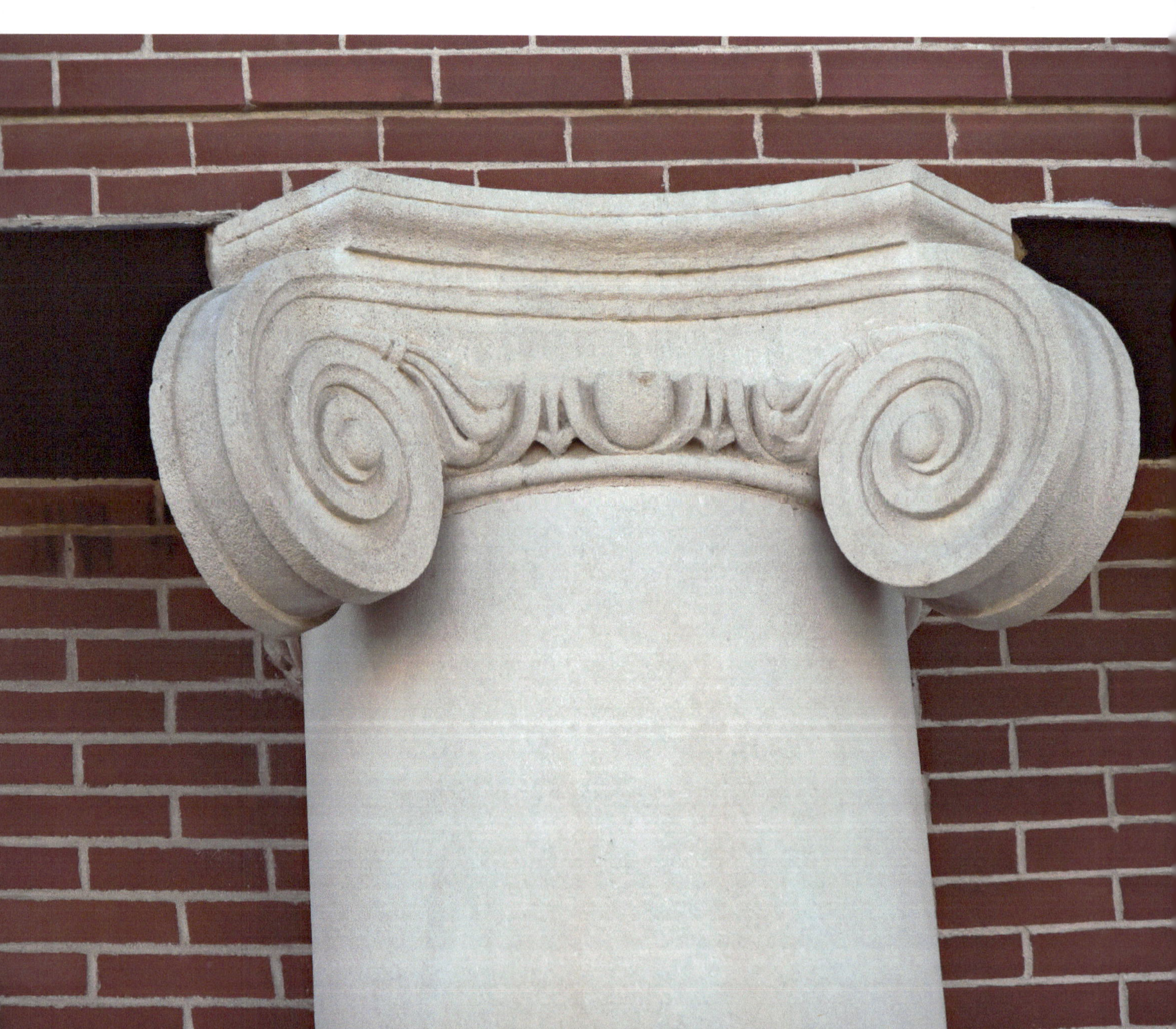

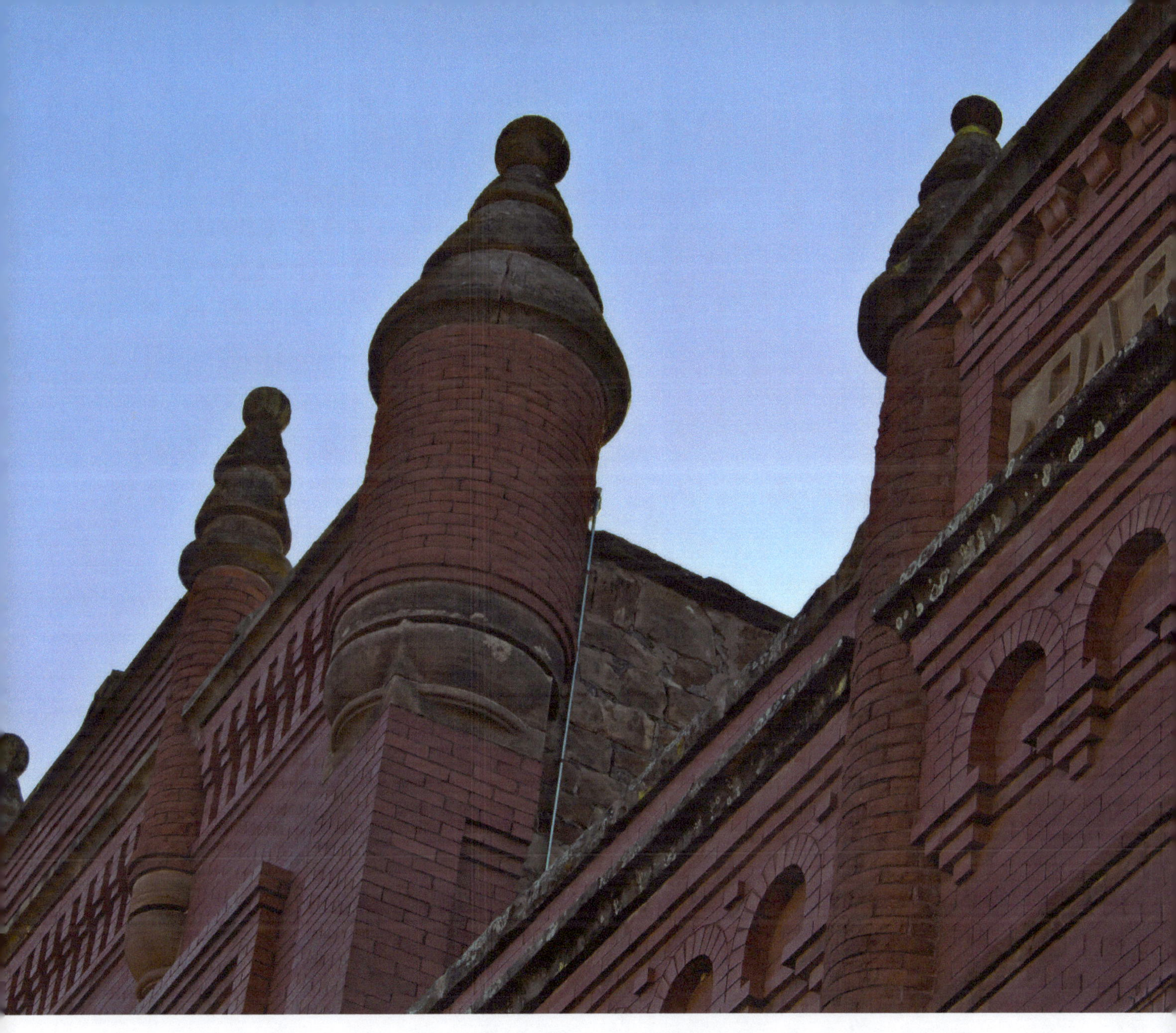

While at the square in the middle of town, look up!
I bet you'll be able to find it very quickly!

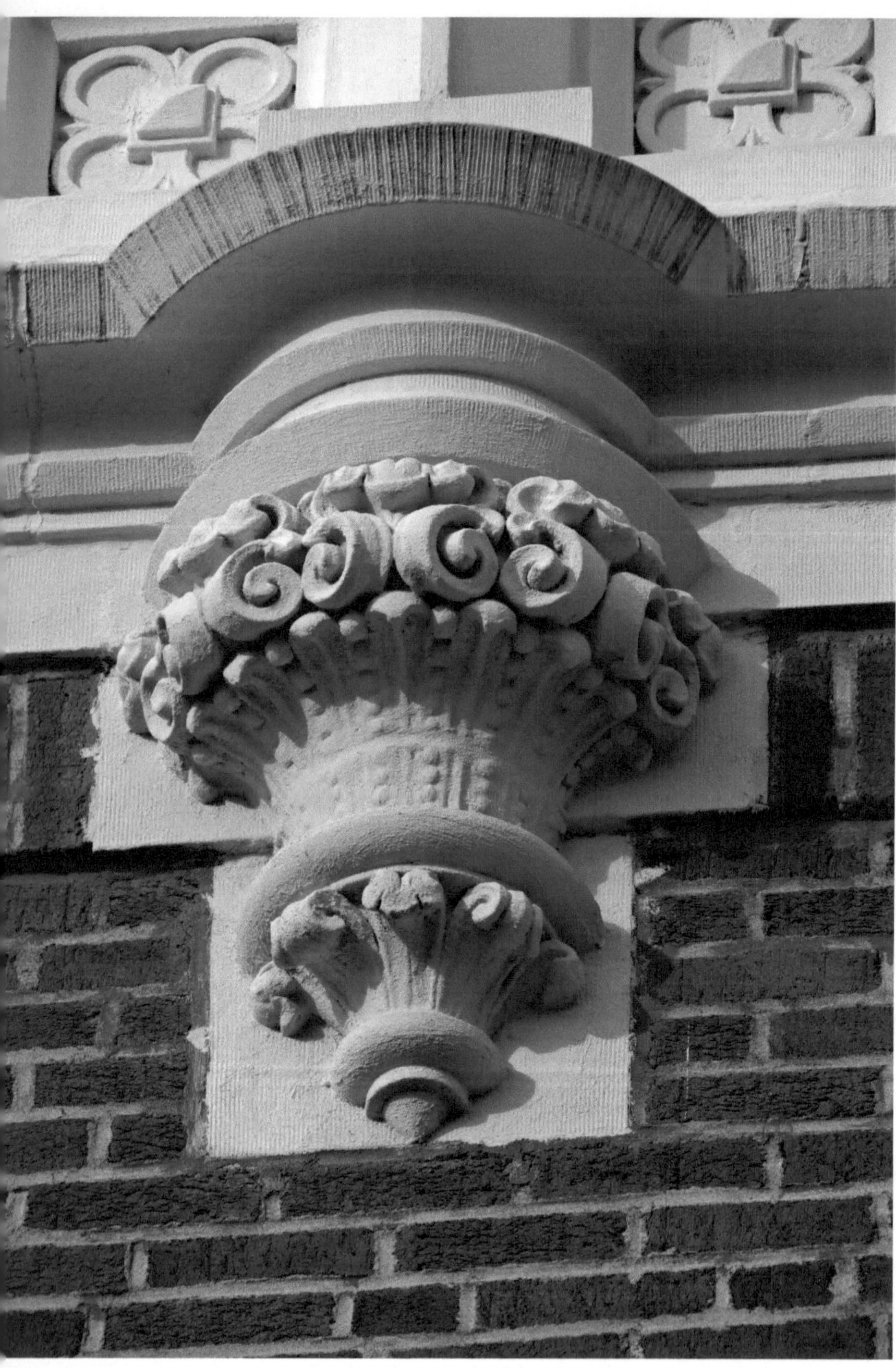

Look at the center of learning – secondary level. You'll probably have to look a bit, but it is there.

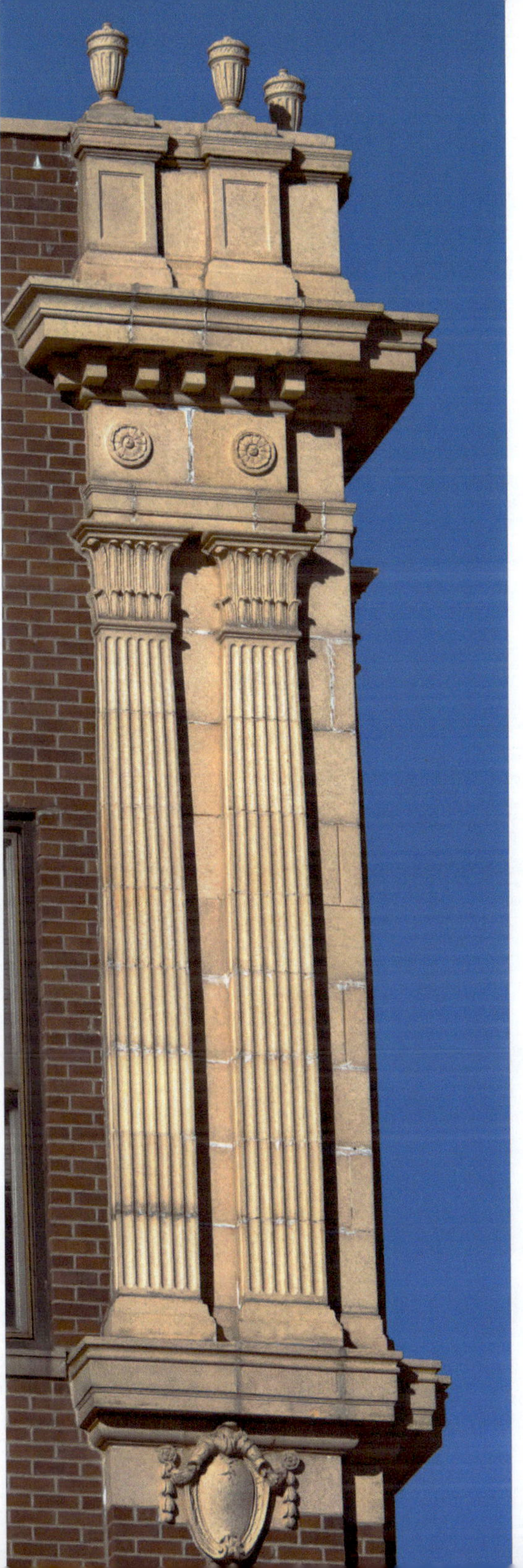

**Look above
the Law
Offices on
5th Street.**

Easy, easy, center of town.

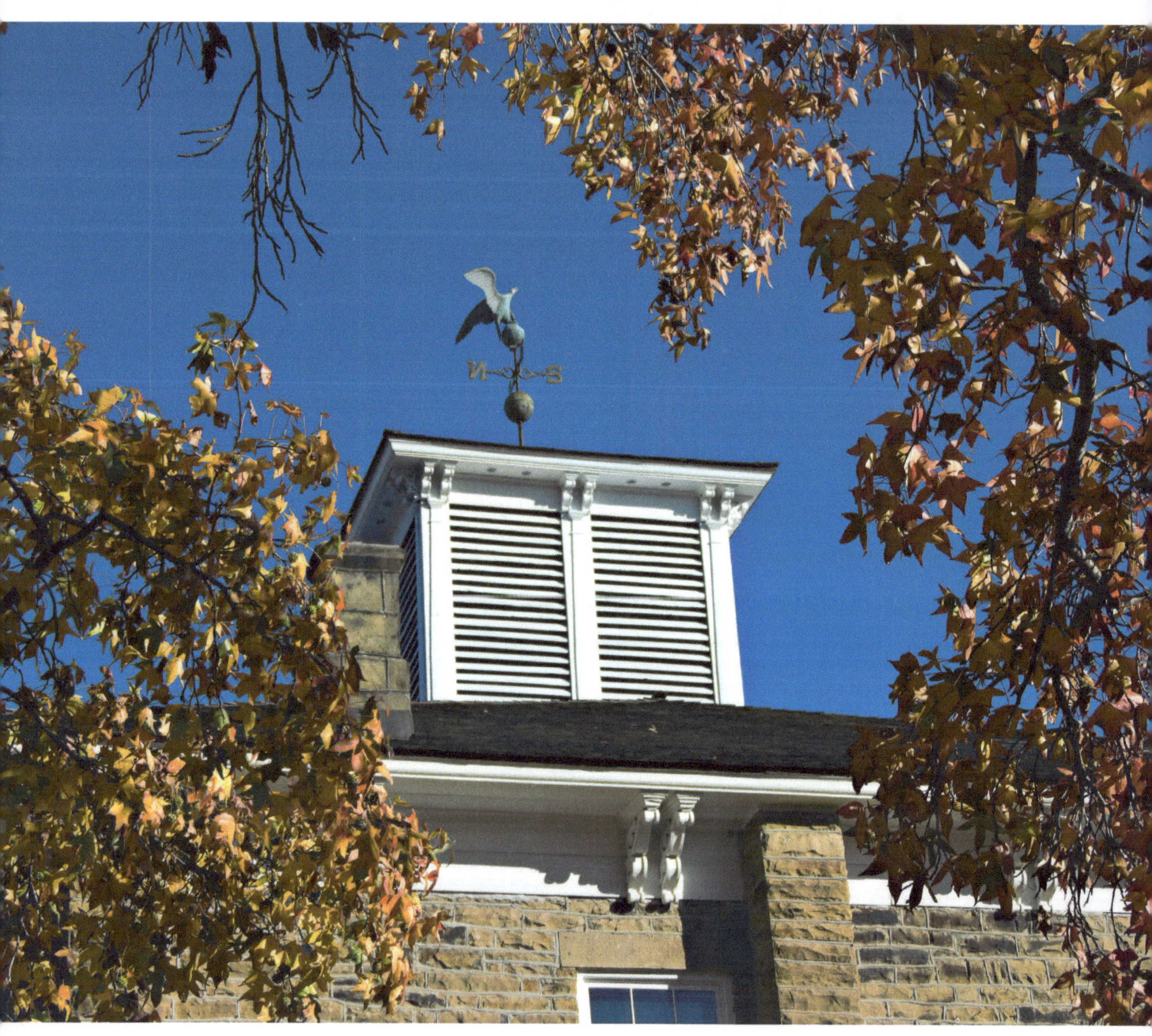

Look to the Law Offices again – on Grand Avenue.

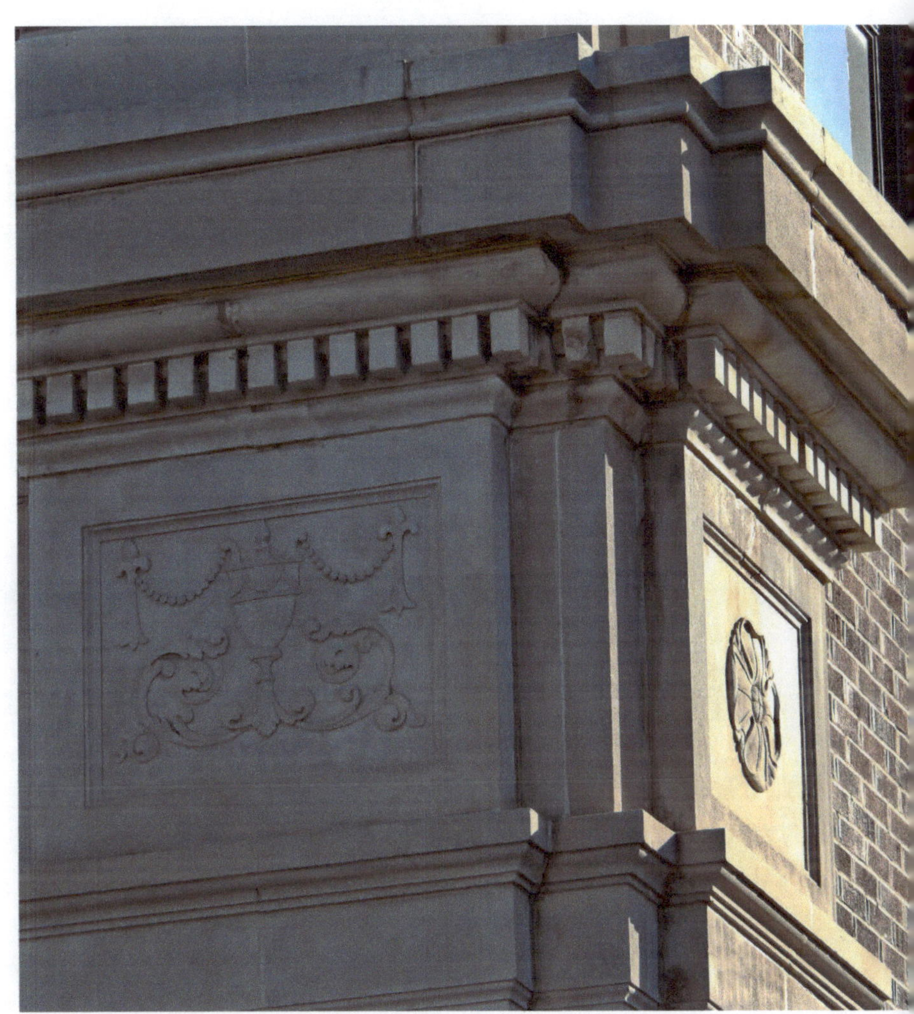

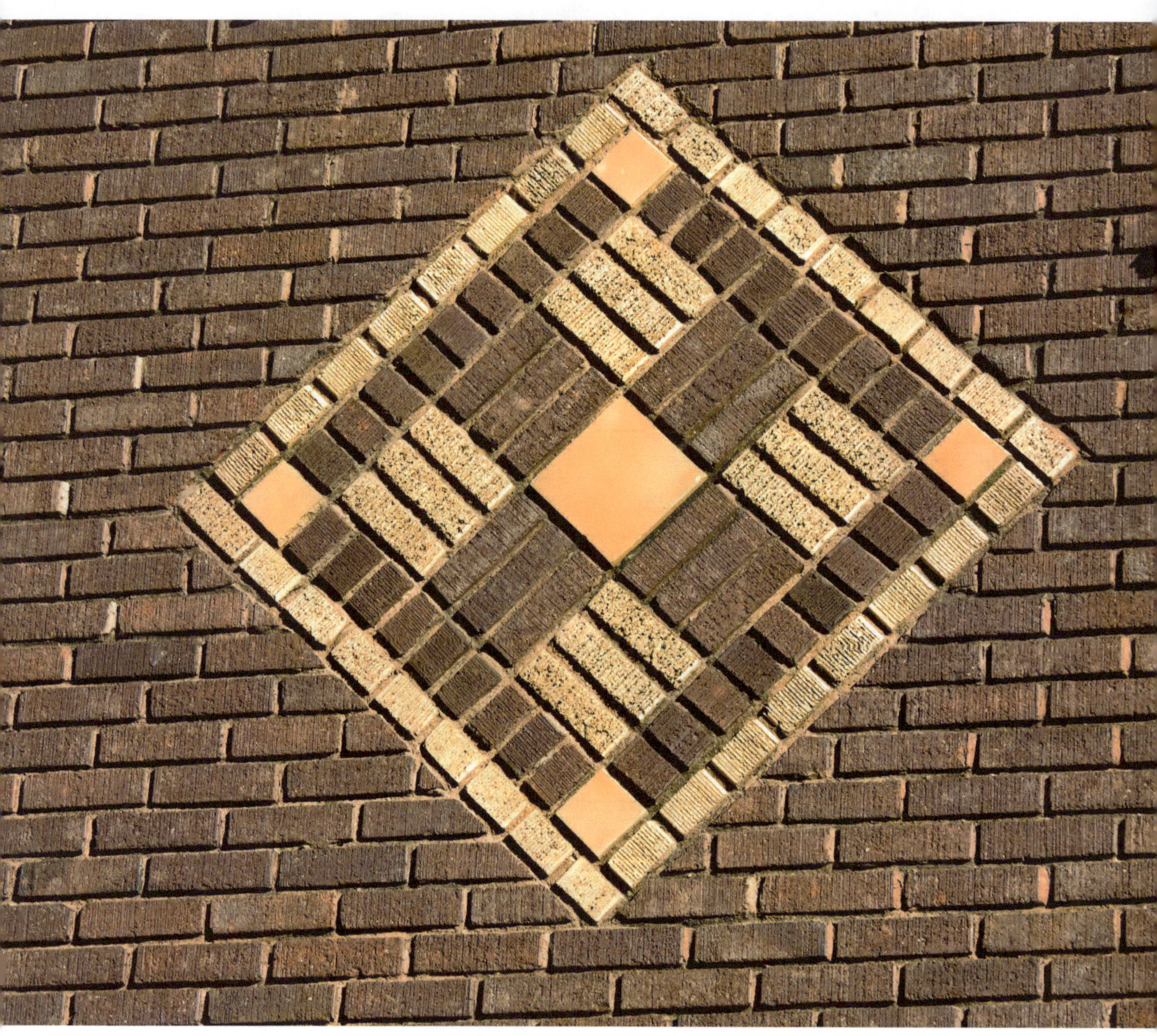

Look for this one near the cleaner's shop.

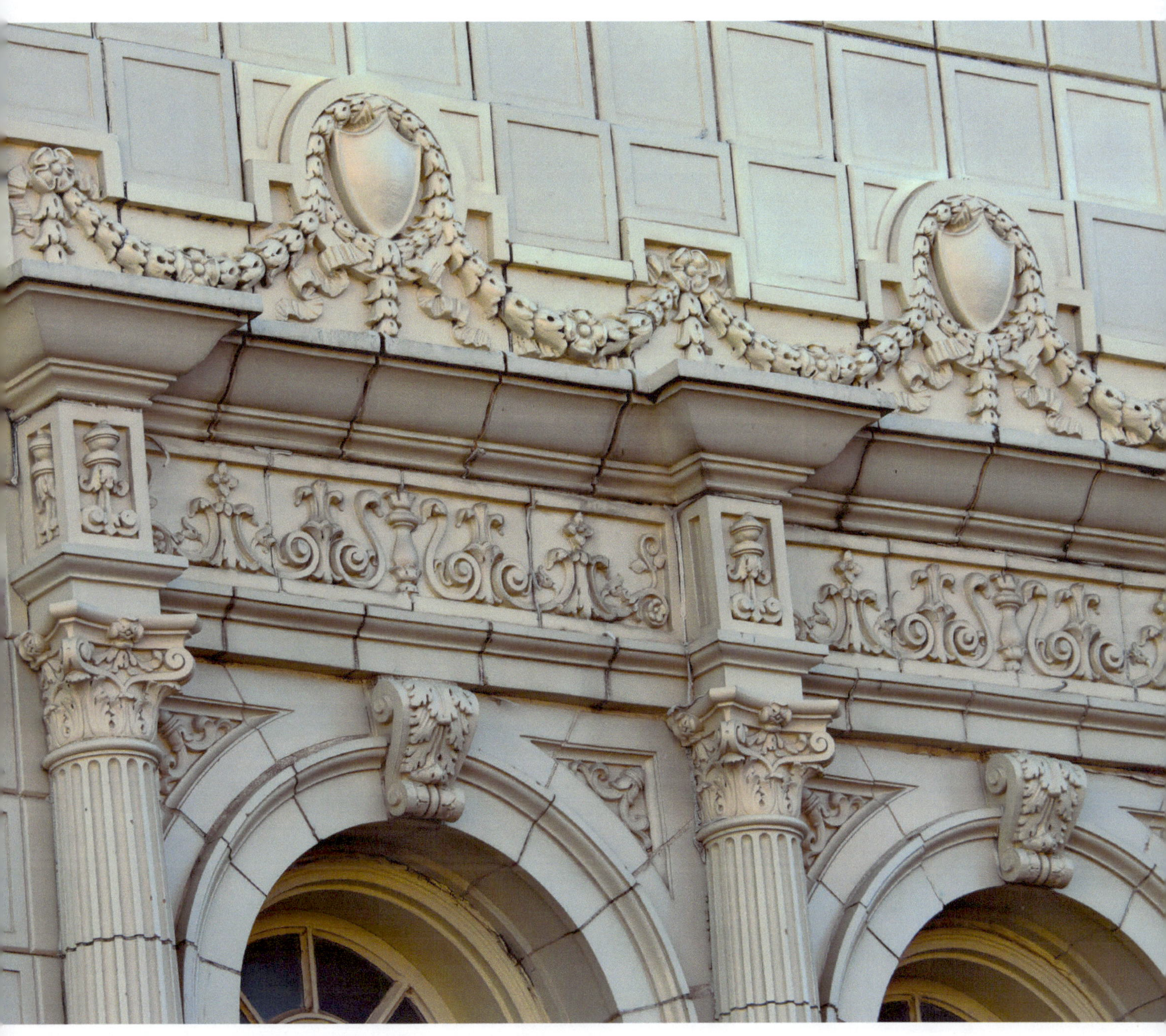

You'll find this one on 7th Street near the square.

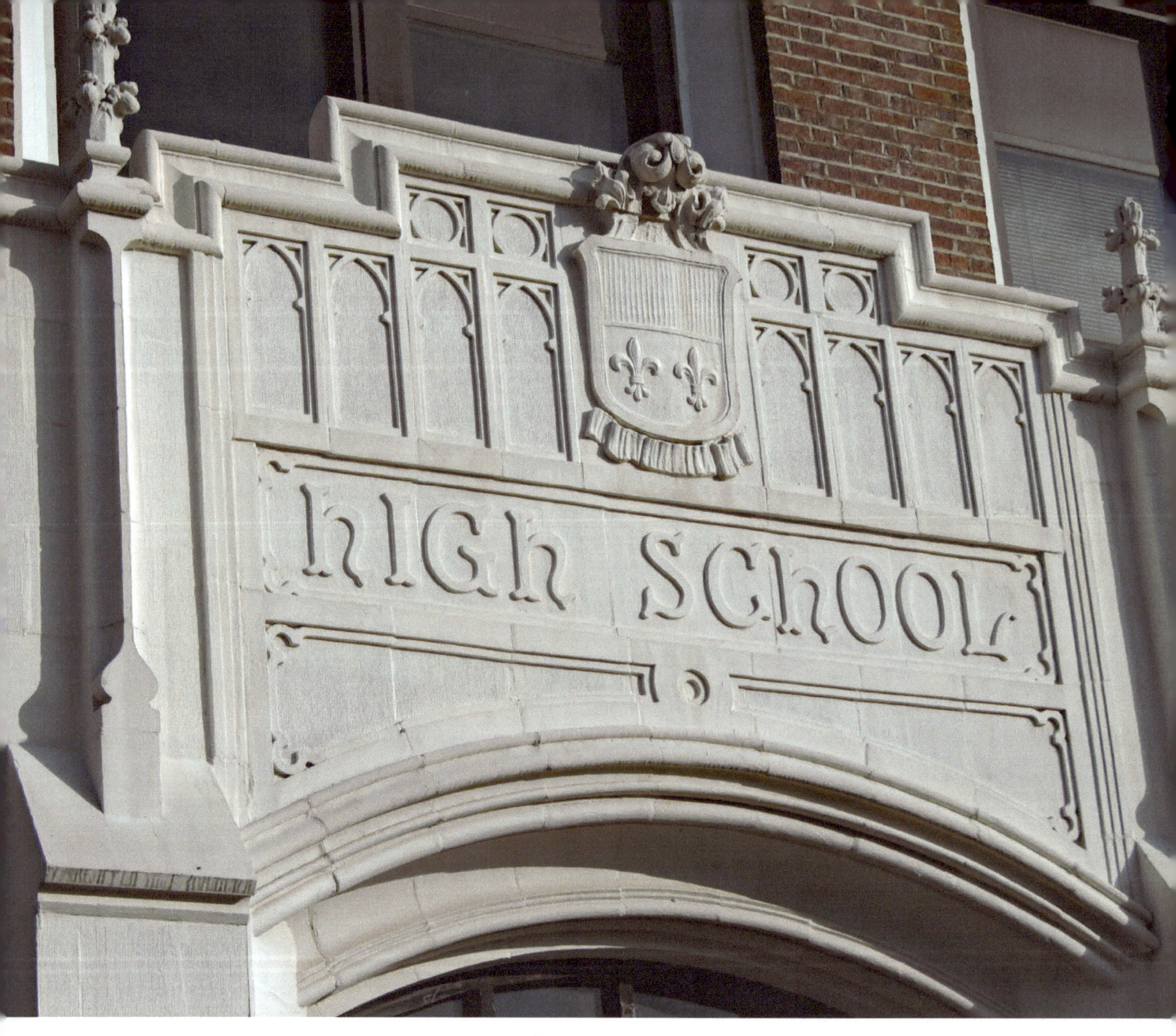

Easy one – the photo itself is a dead giveaway.

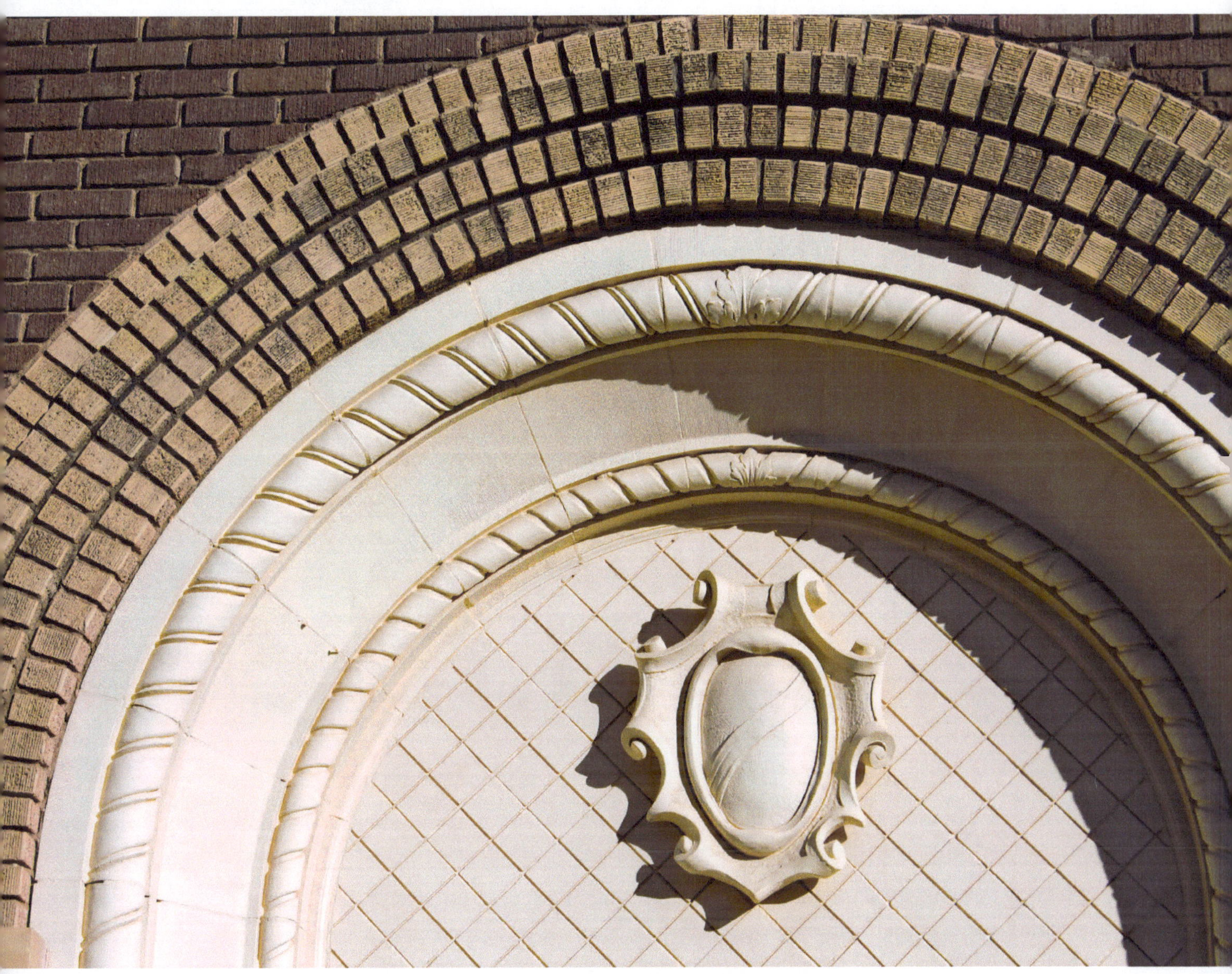

Look on South Grand Avenue near the cleaner's.

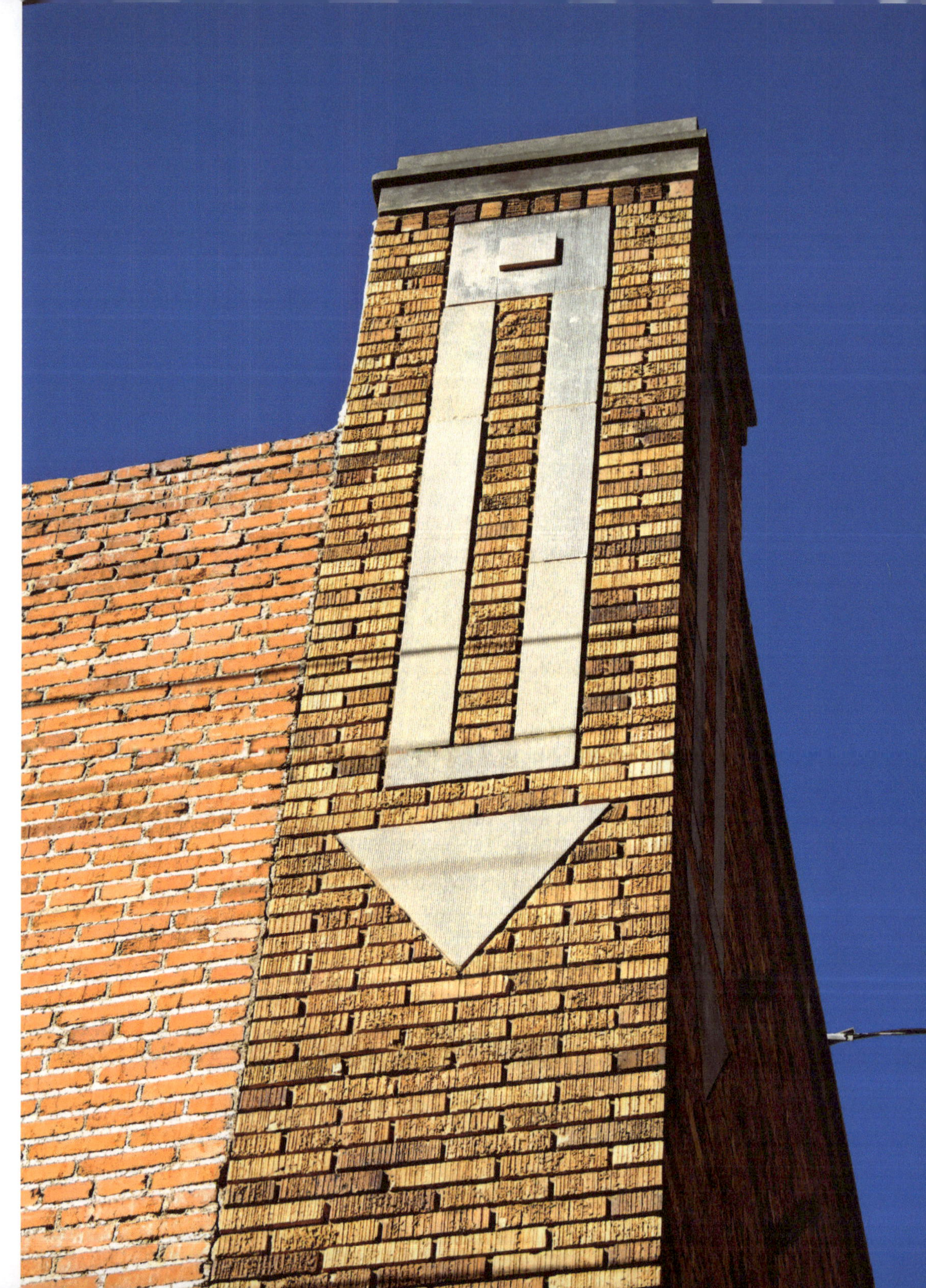

**Once
again,
look
behind
the
cleaner's!**

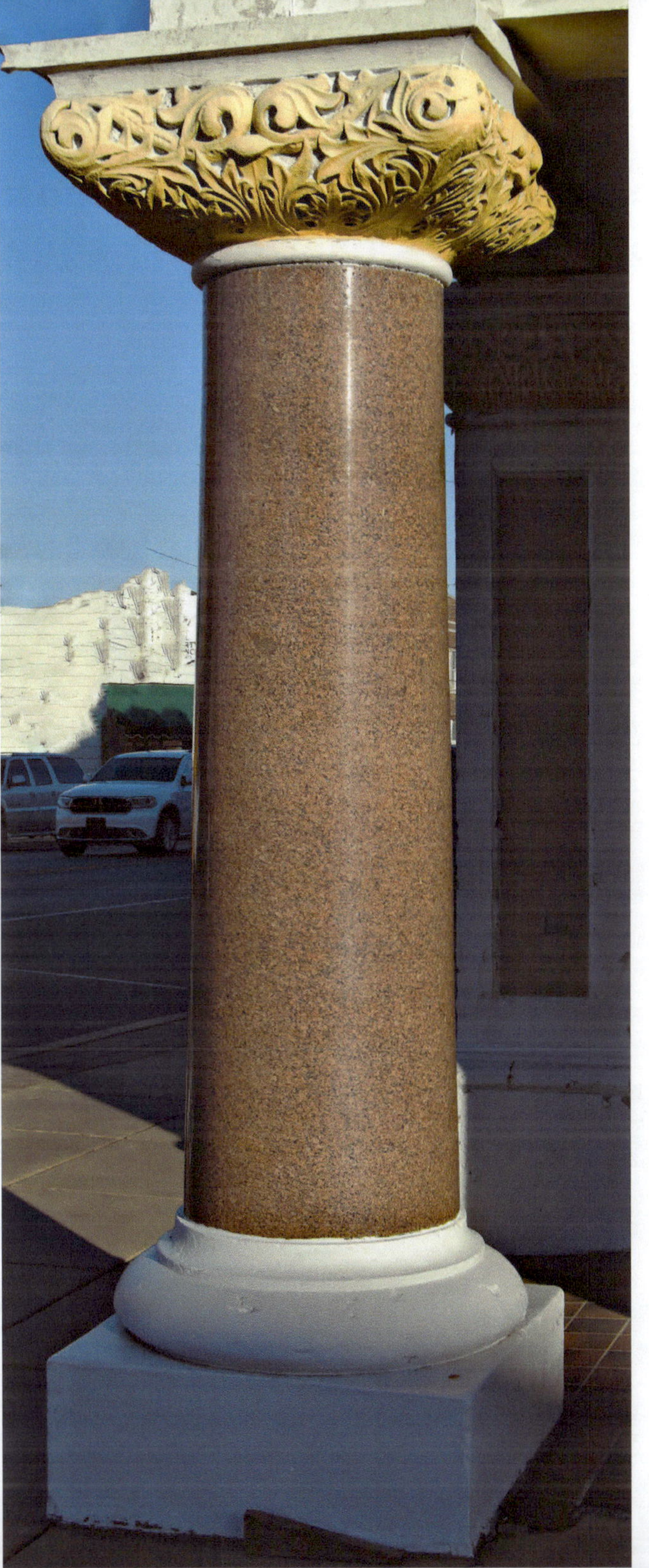

Look across the street from the Pawn Shop.

This one may be a bit harder to find. Look on Main Street, about a block east of the square.

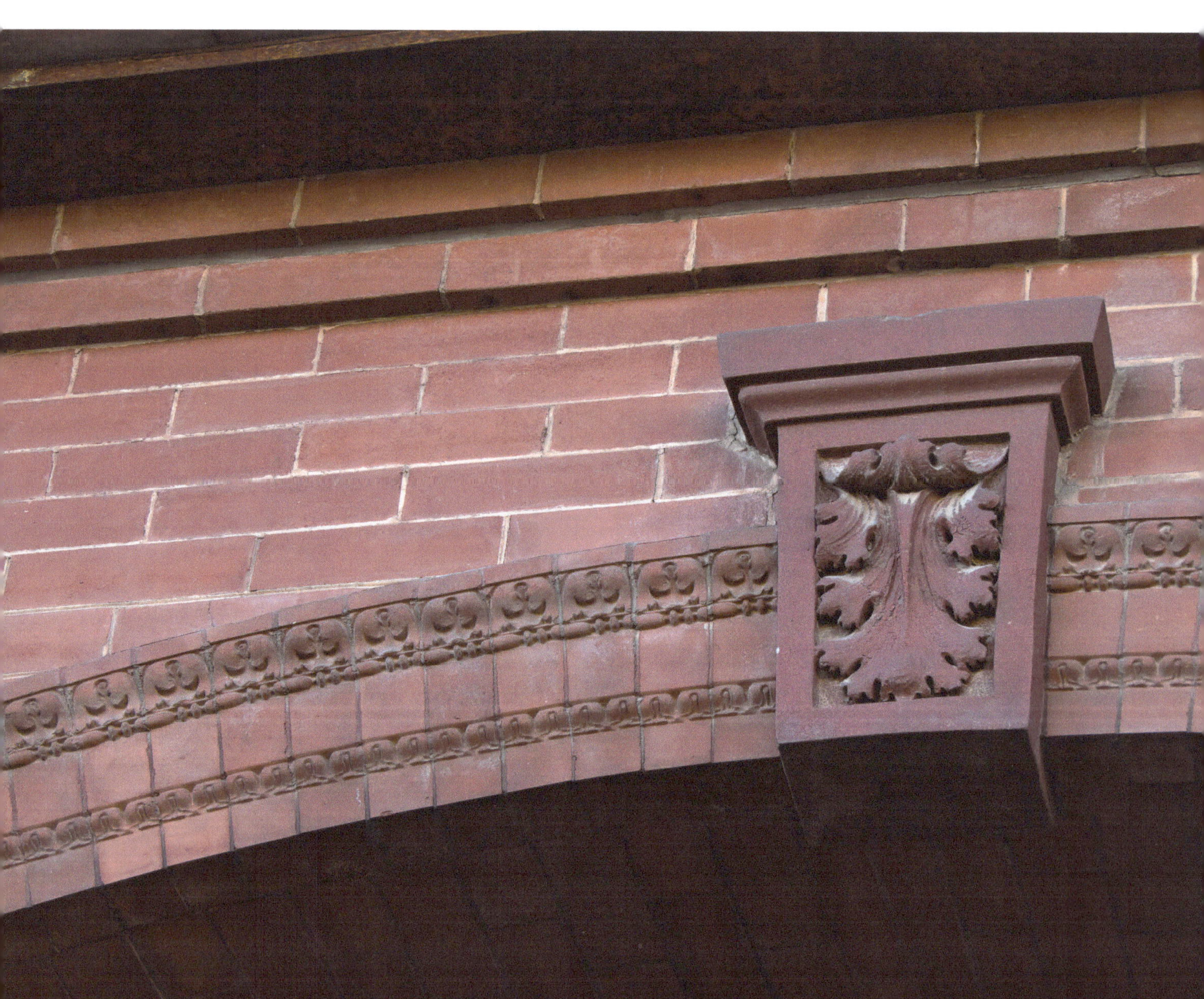

You might find this one about Central and Main.

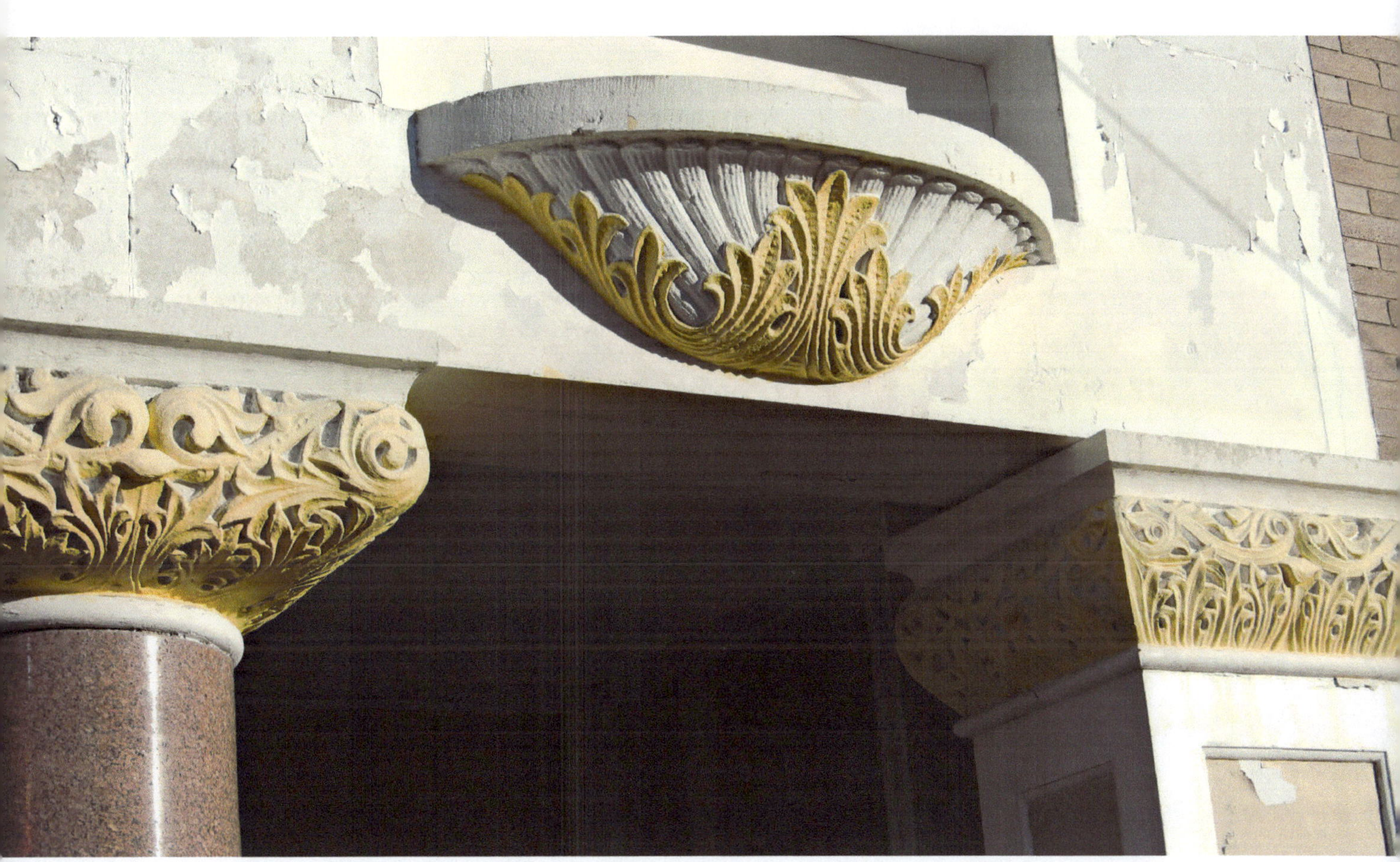

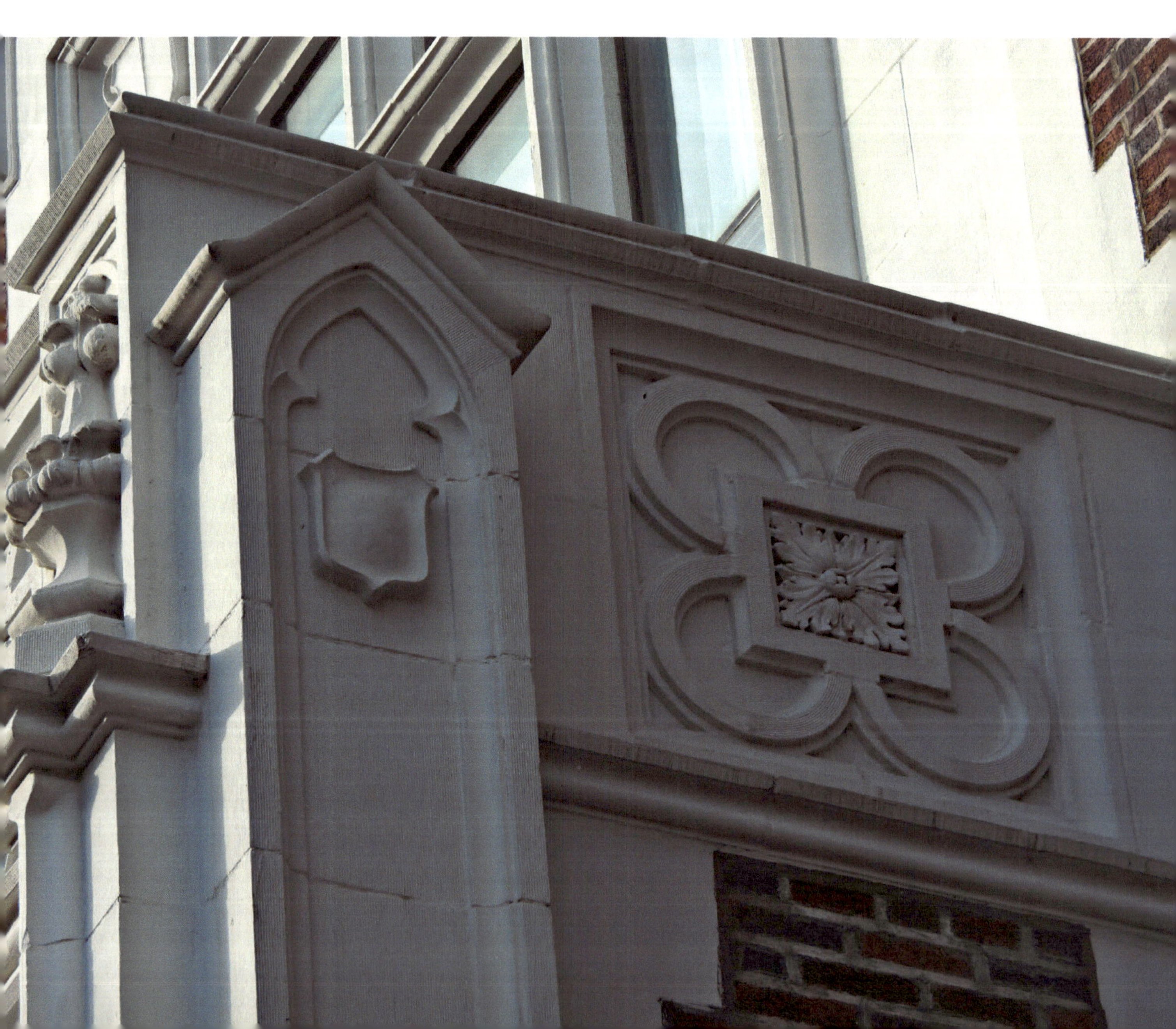

Back to the center of learning again.

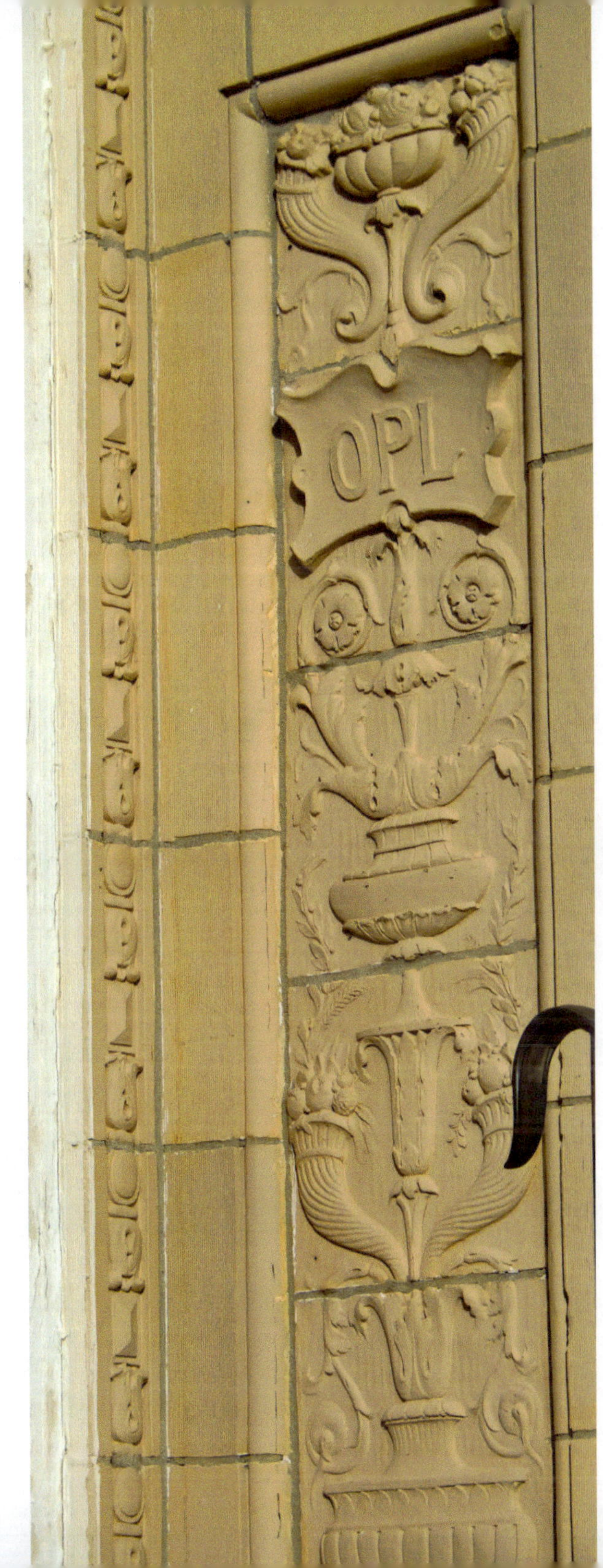

They have
all kinds of
books in
this place.

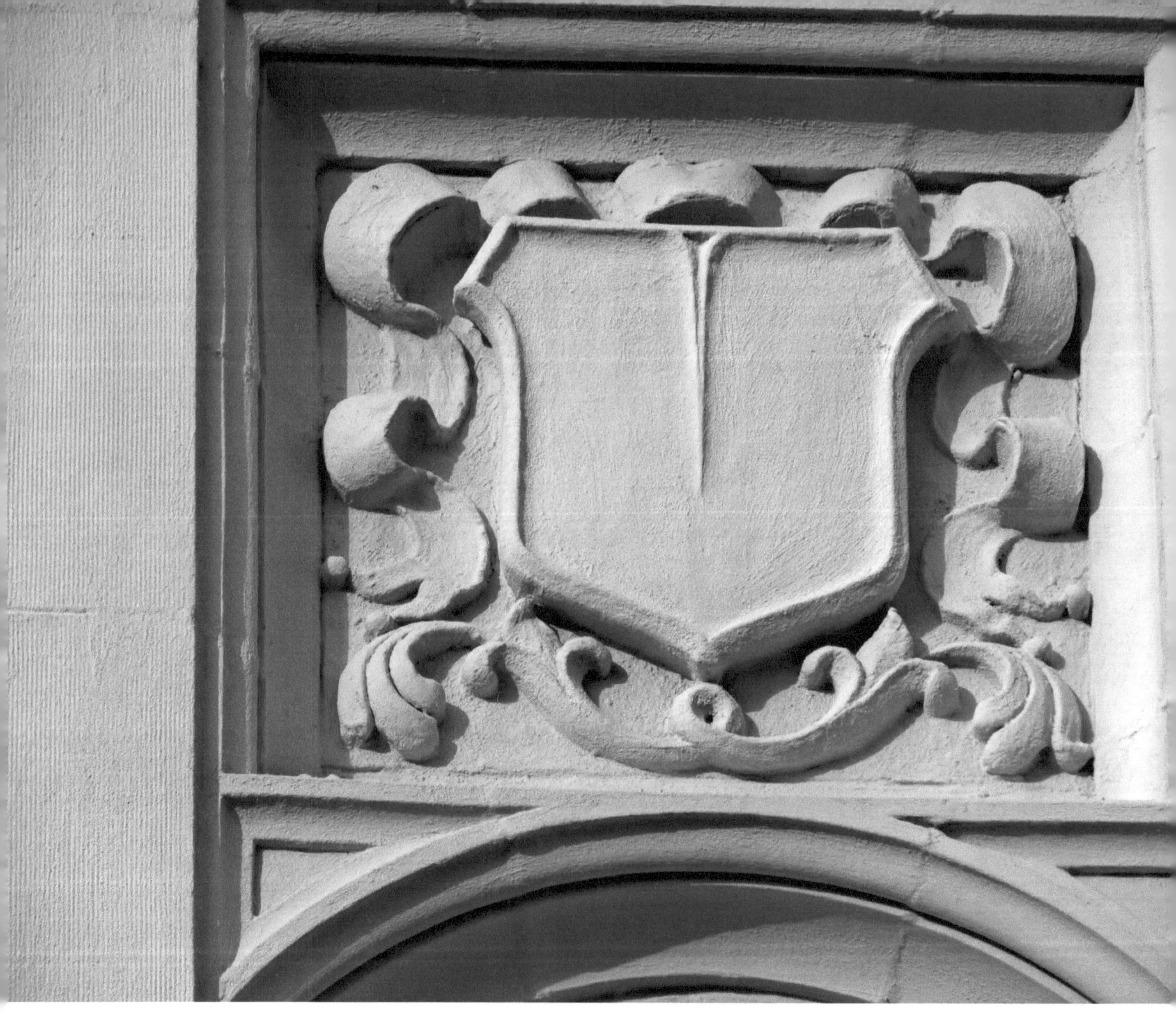

A shield of learning.

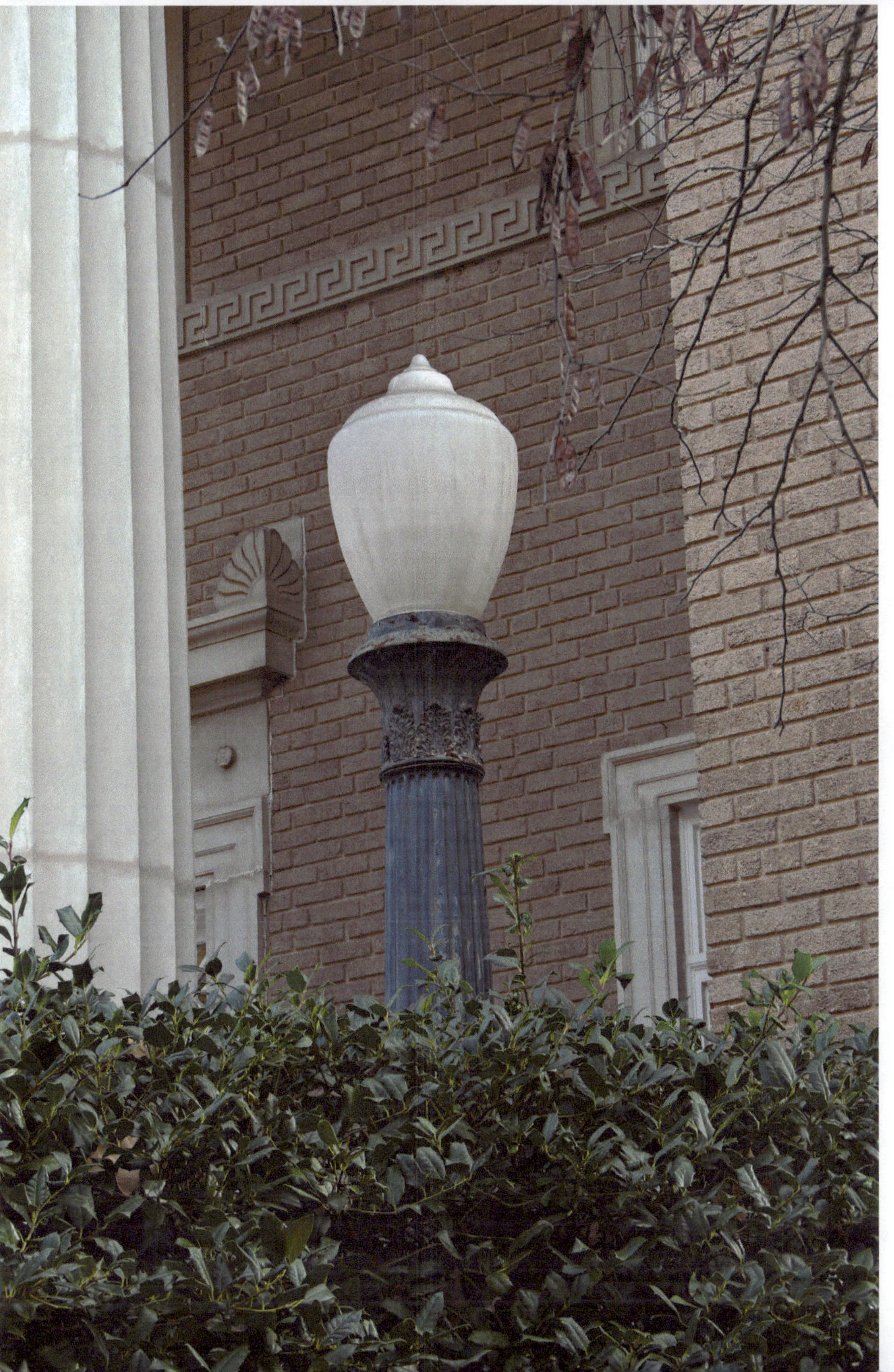

Go south on Seminole and look for the large Greek pillars. You may find it there.

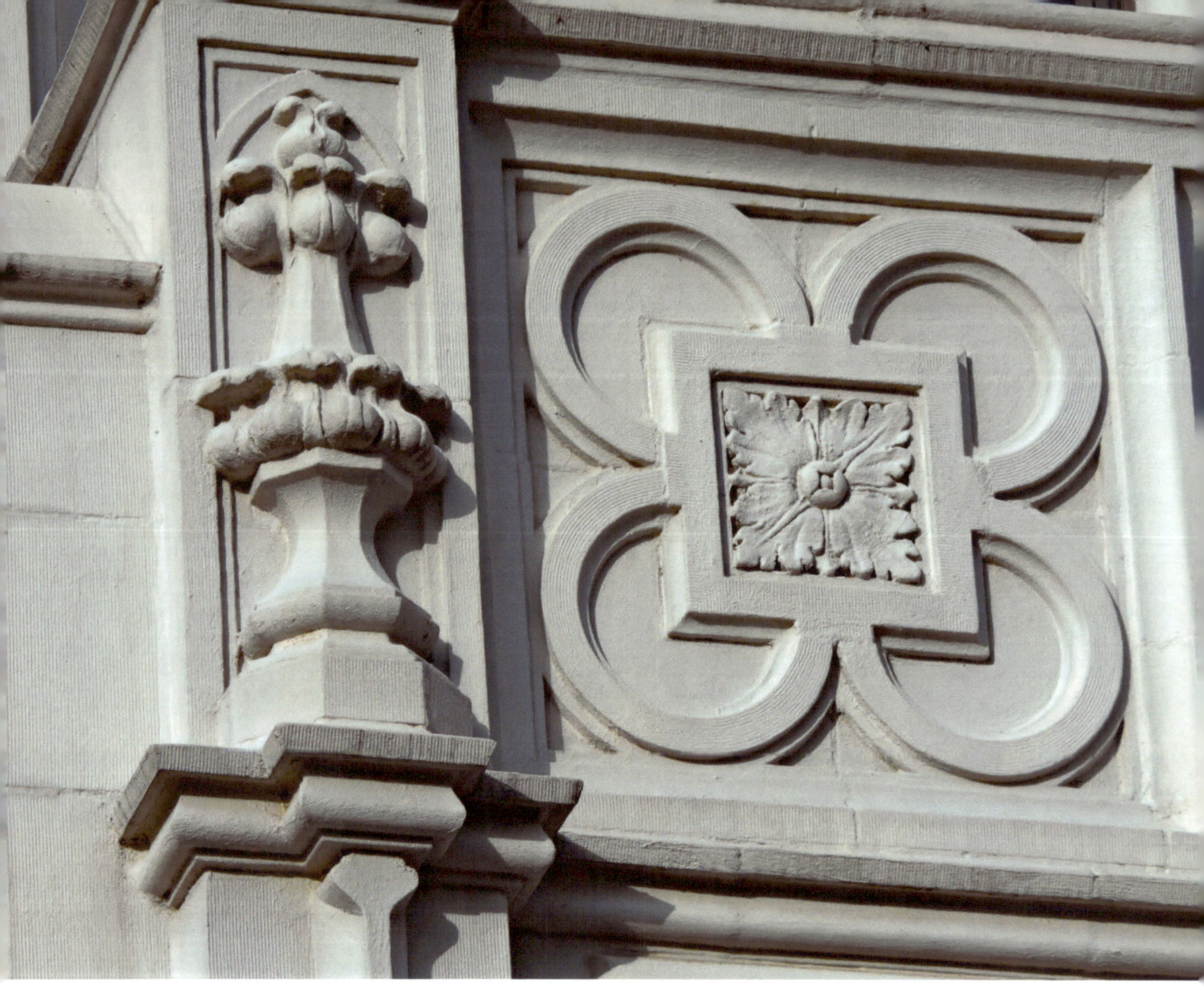

This center of learning is getting a lot of attention.

**At the Council House, look up and all around.
If you never noticed before, we are protected by lions.**

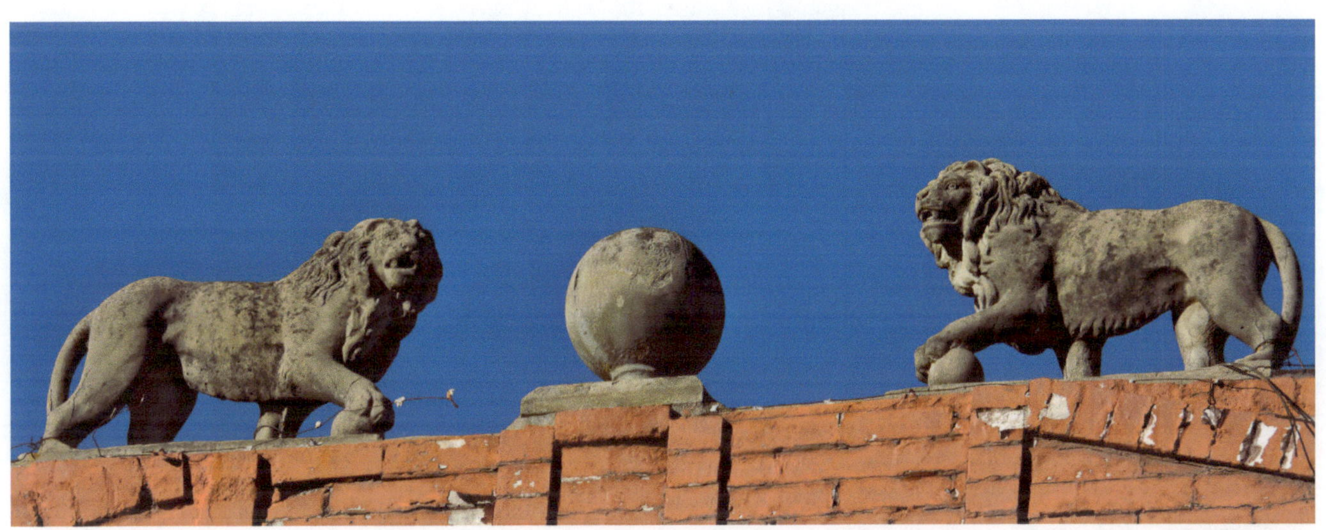

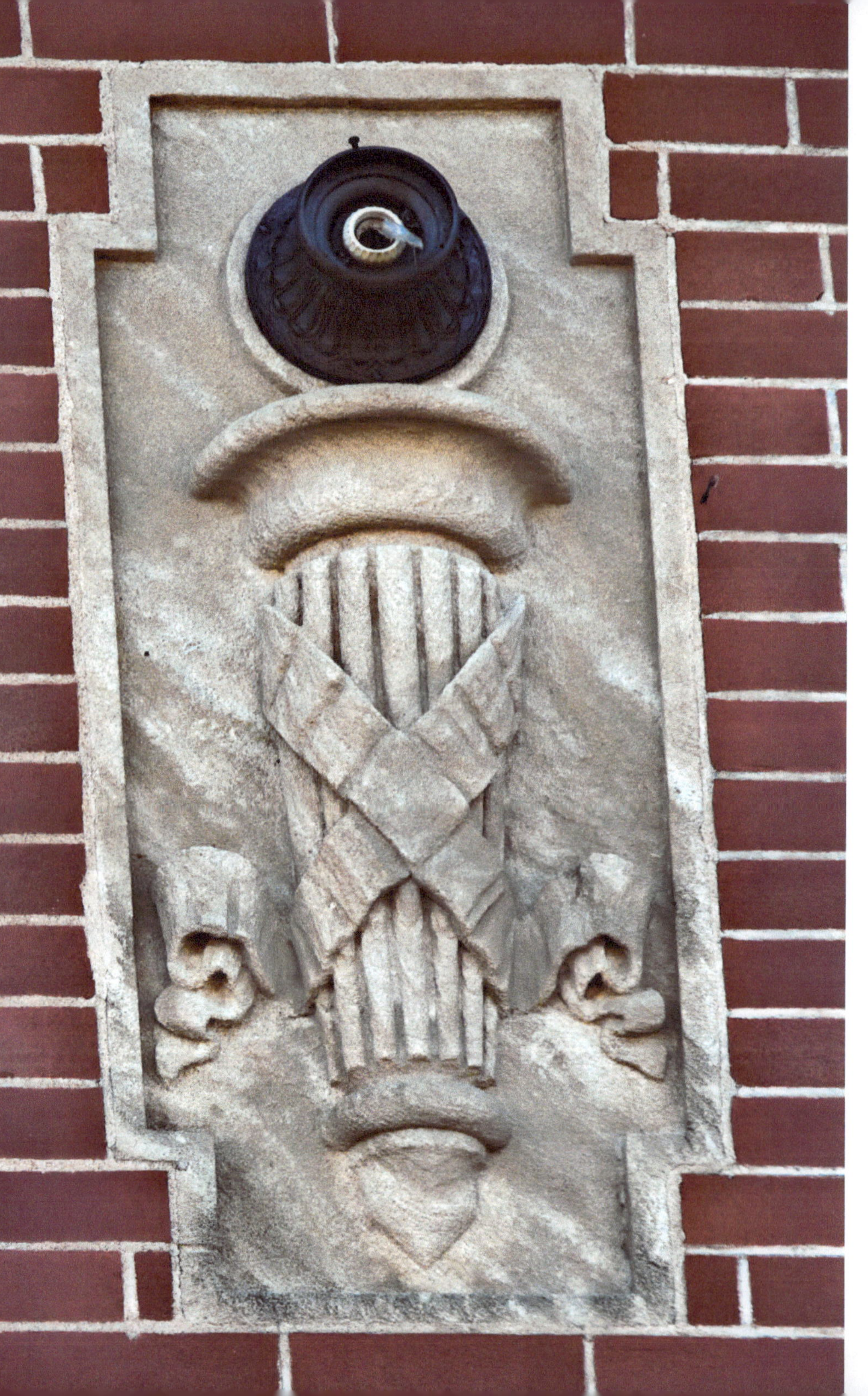

If you need
to go before
the judge,
you might
find this
artifact on
the wall.

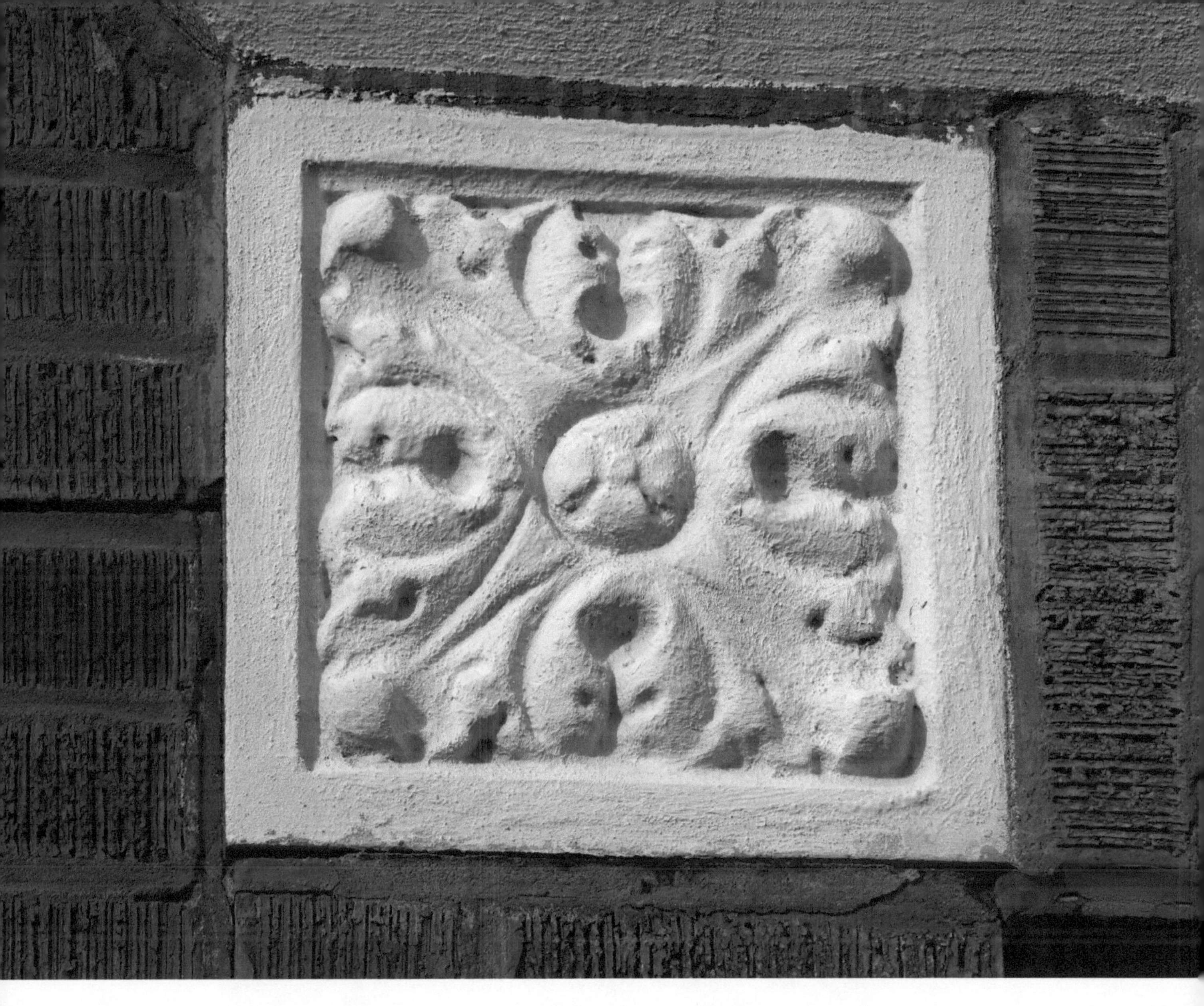

A lot of music gets practiced here at
the learning center.

Another grand old church of Okmulgee displays these roof top ornaments.

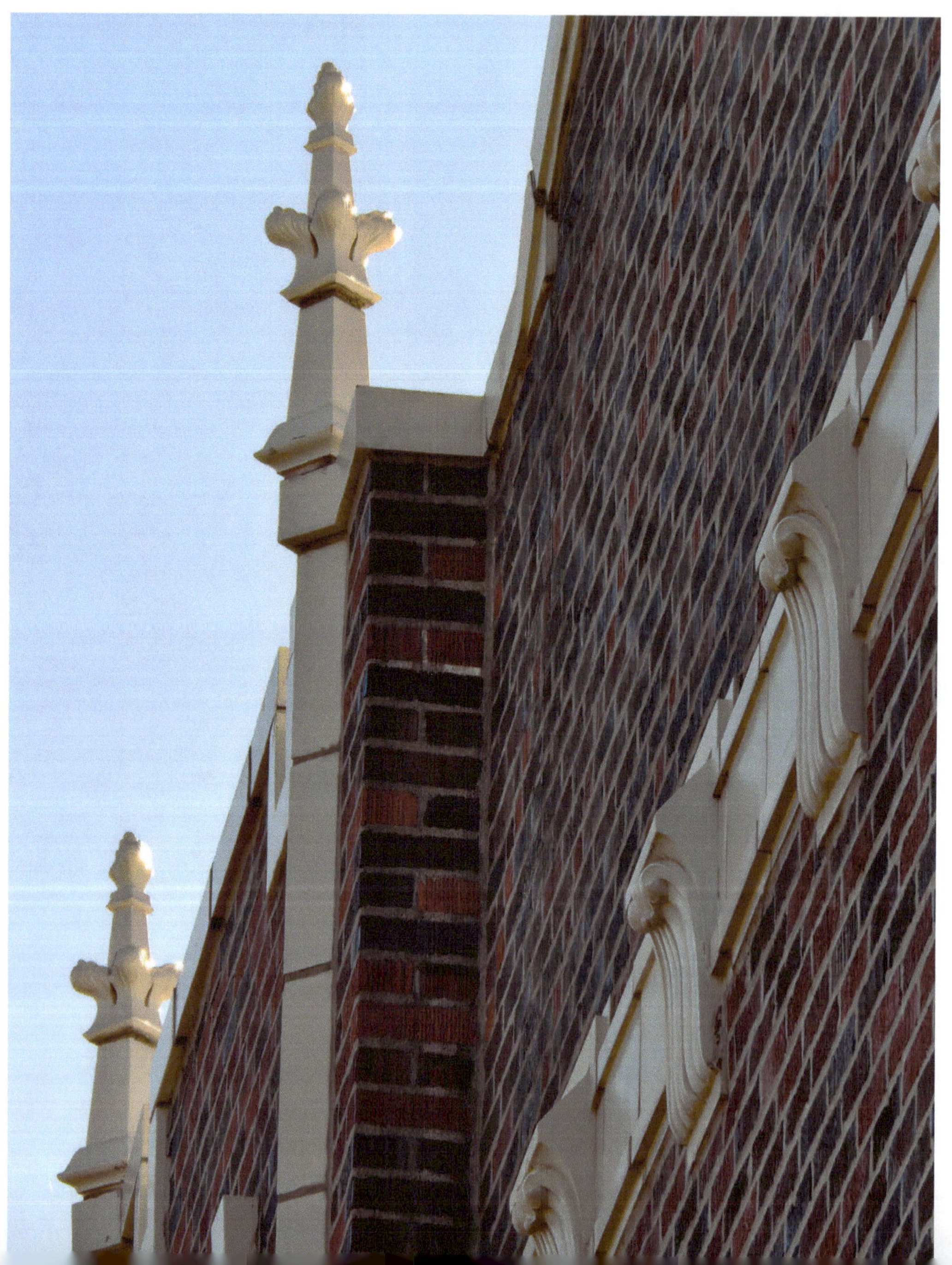

Once again, across from
the Council House –
different corner.

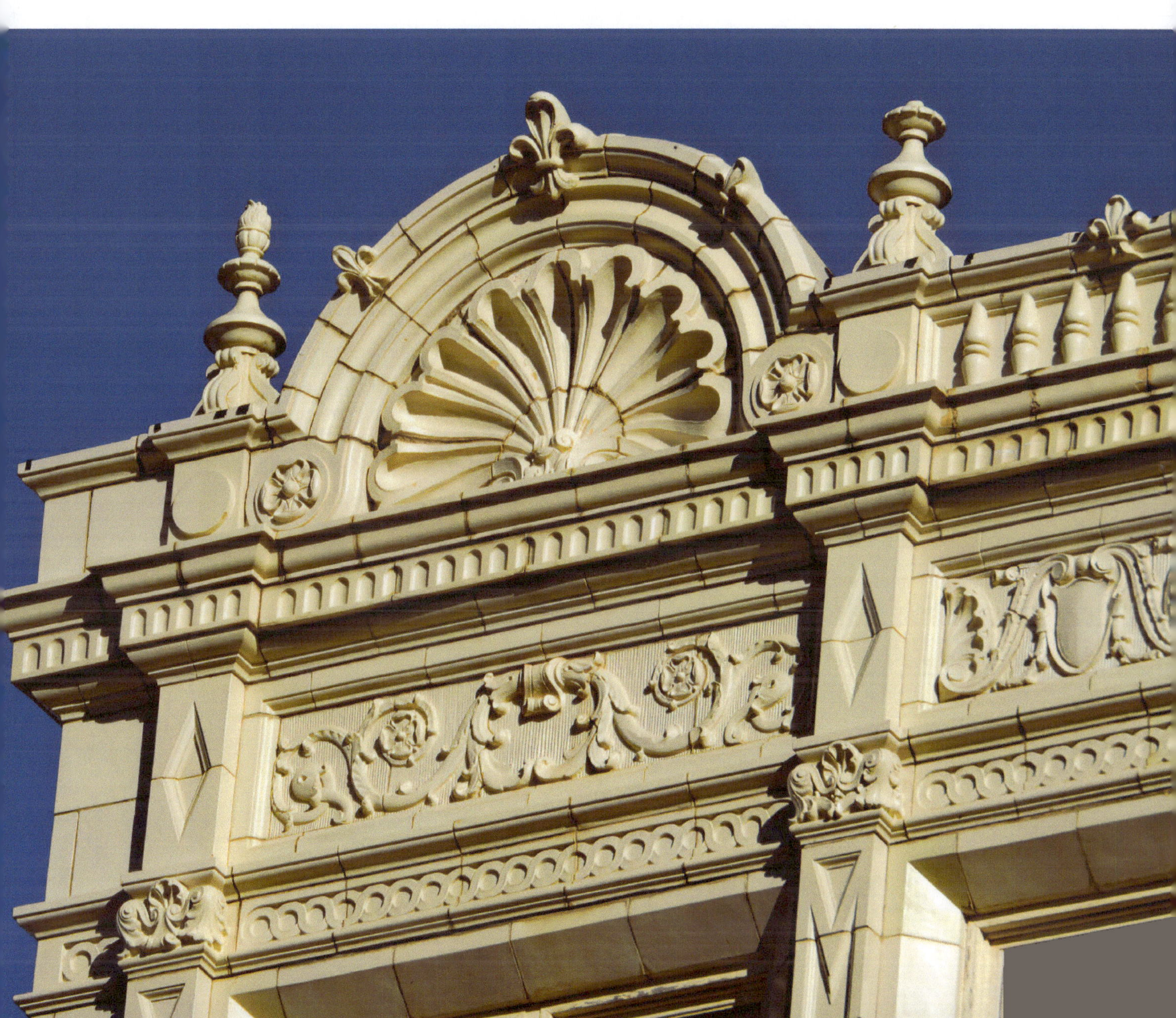

You may have seen this before, when you were looking for columns and a lamp.

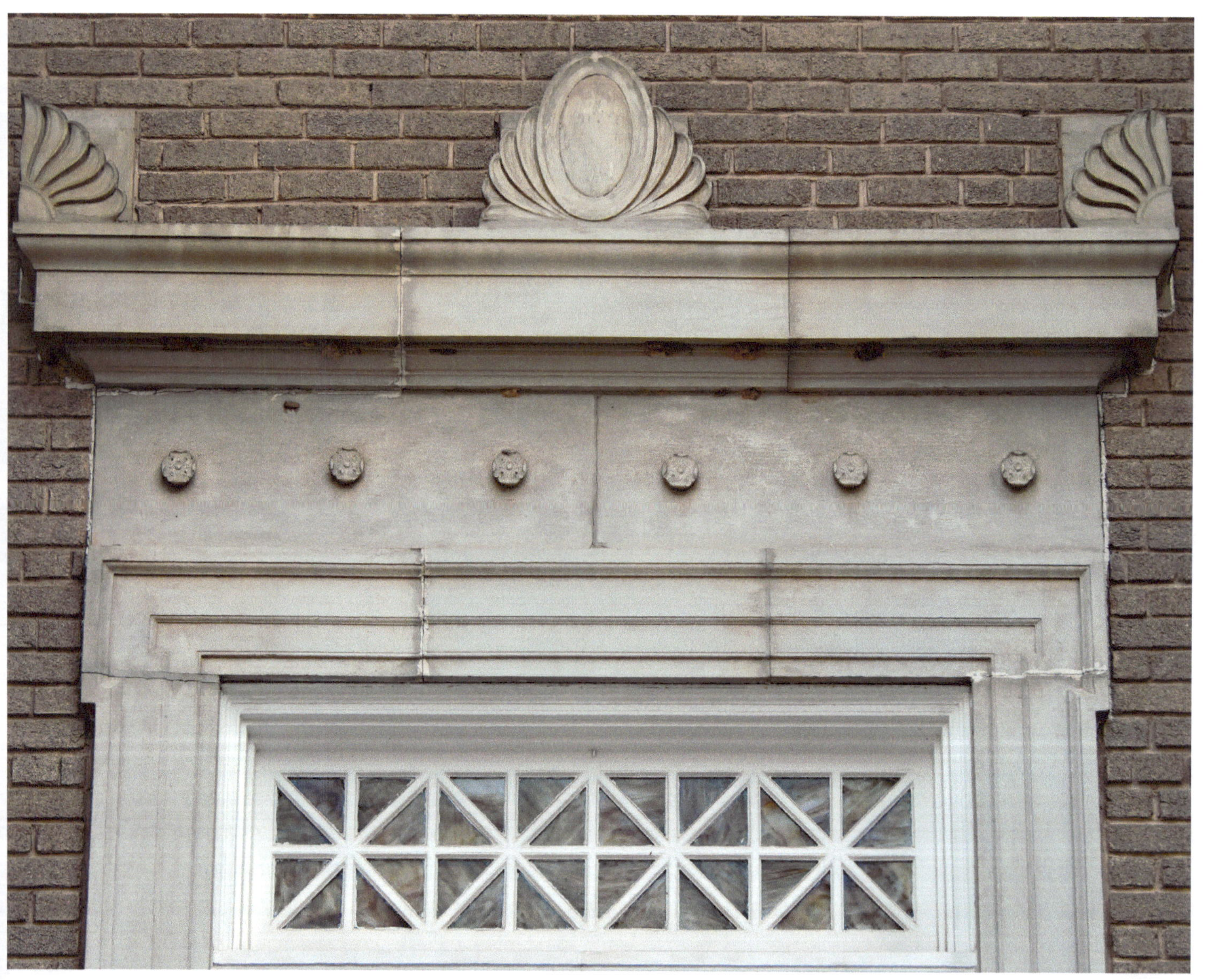

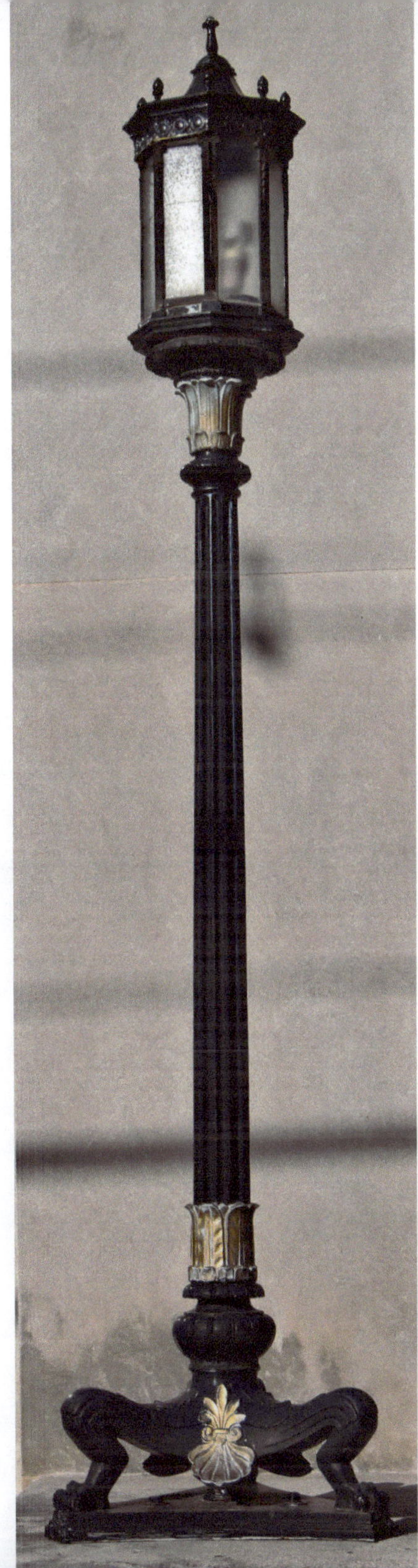

Need a
Passport?
You might
try this
official
Federal
Building.

This one might be a bit of a challenge. In some ways it is kind of hard to spot. Look around the area of Main and Central.

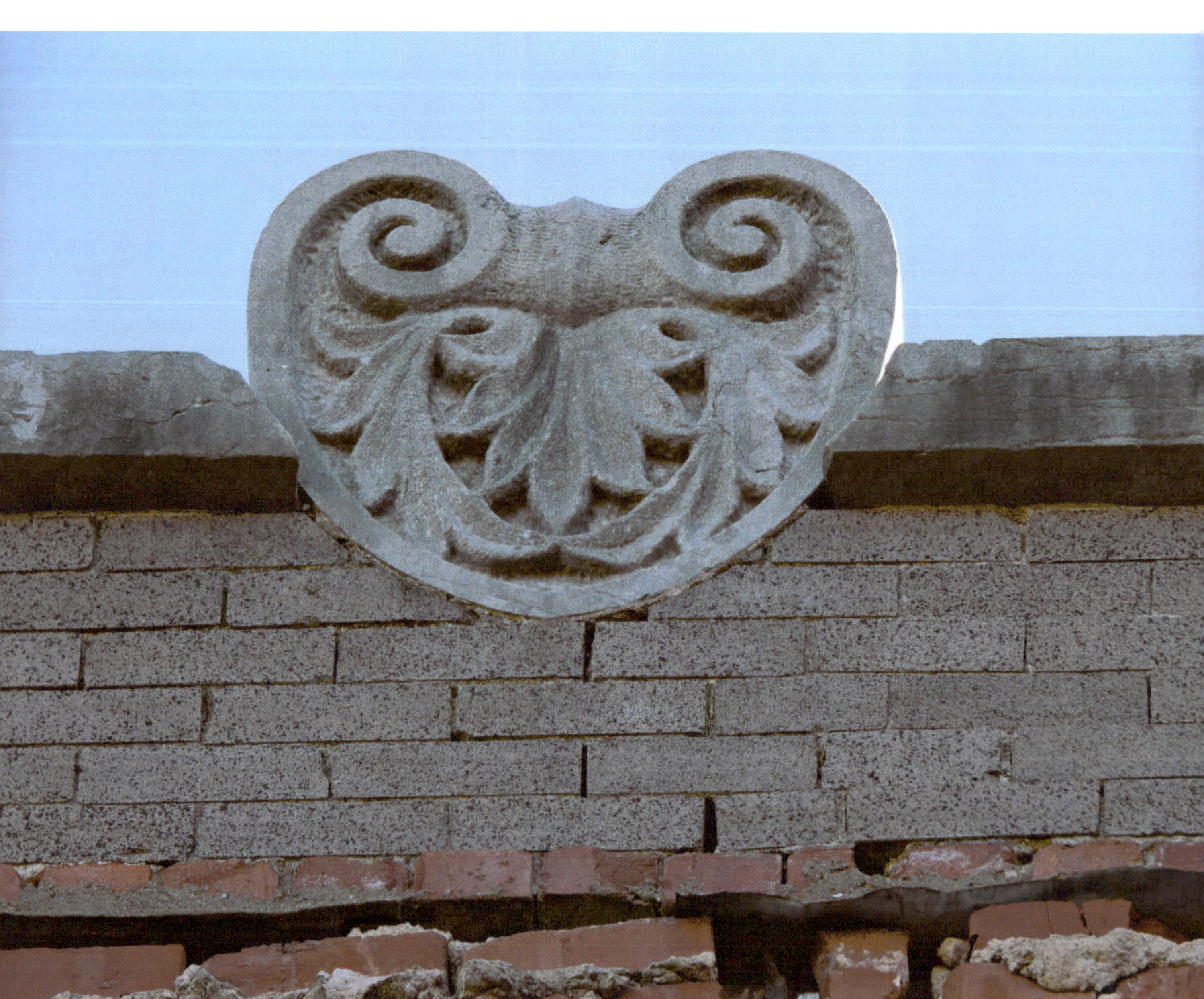

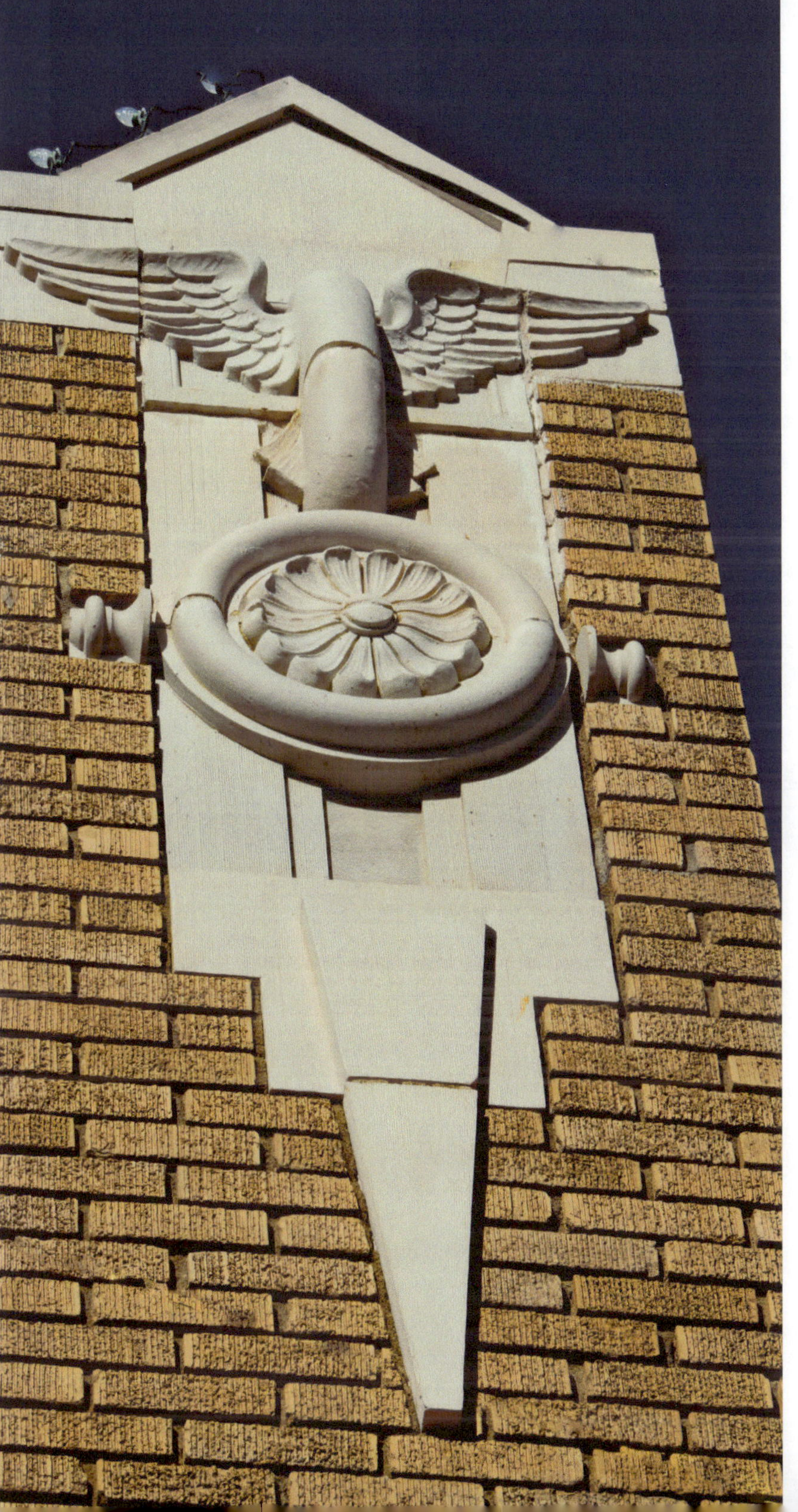

If you can
find the Ford
Lofts, you
can find this
one.

Once again looking above the Law Offices on Grand Avenue.

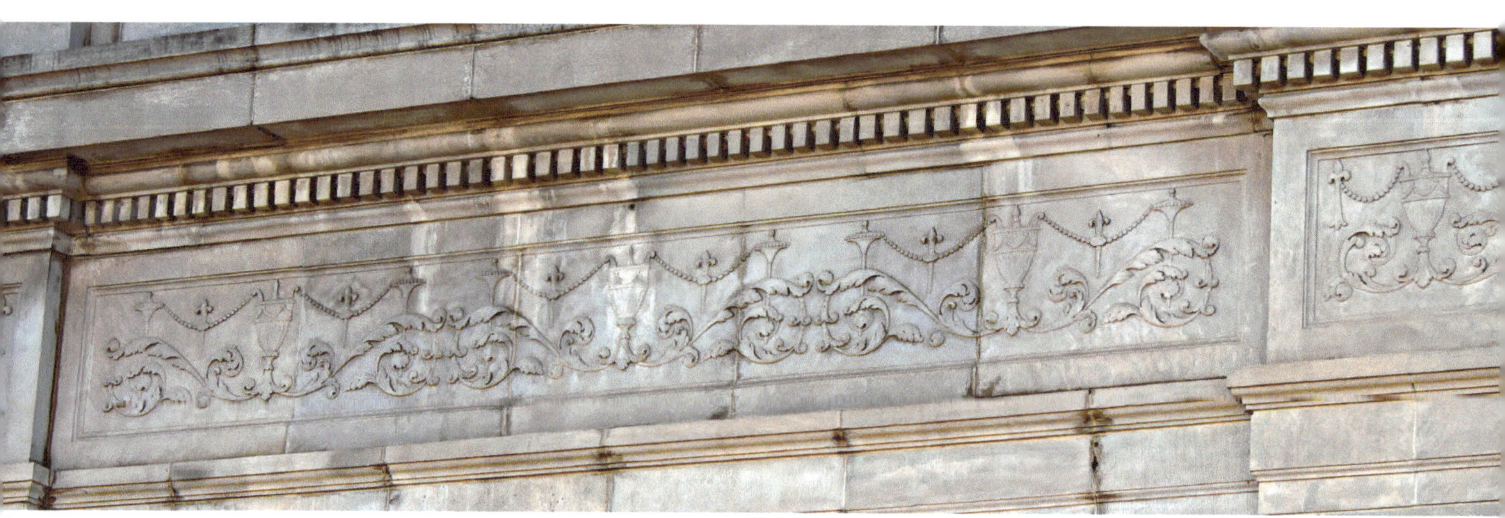

Look around the area of 7ᵗʰ Street and Seminole.

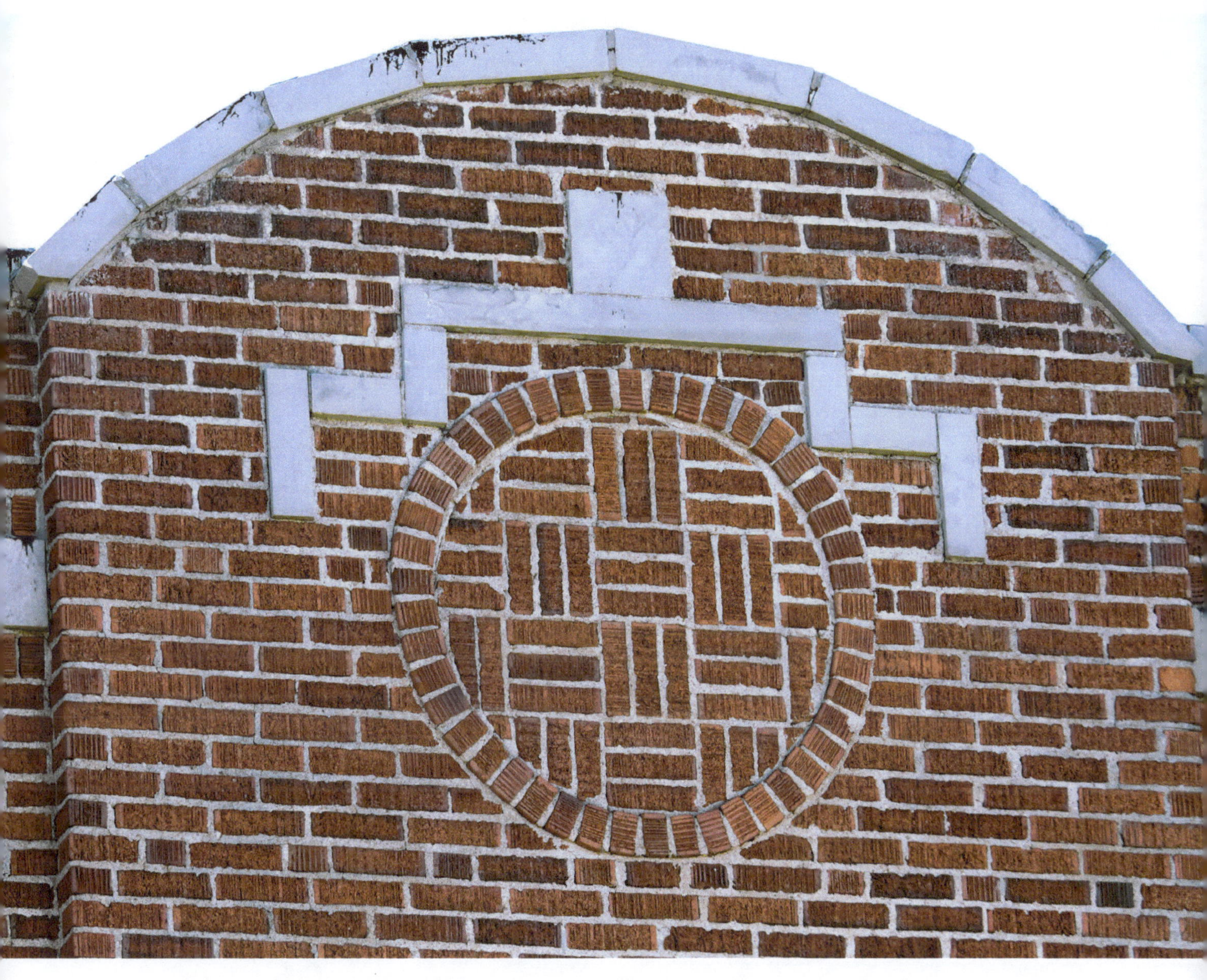

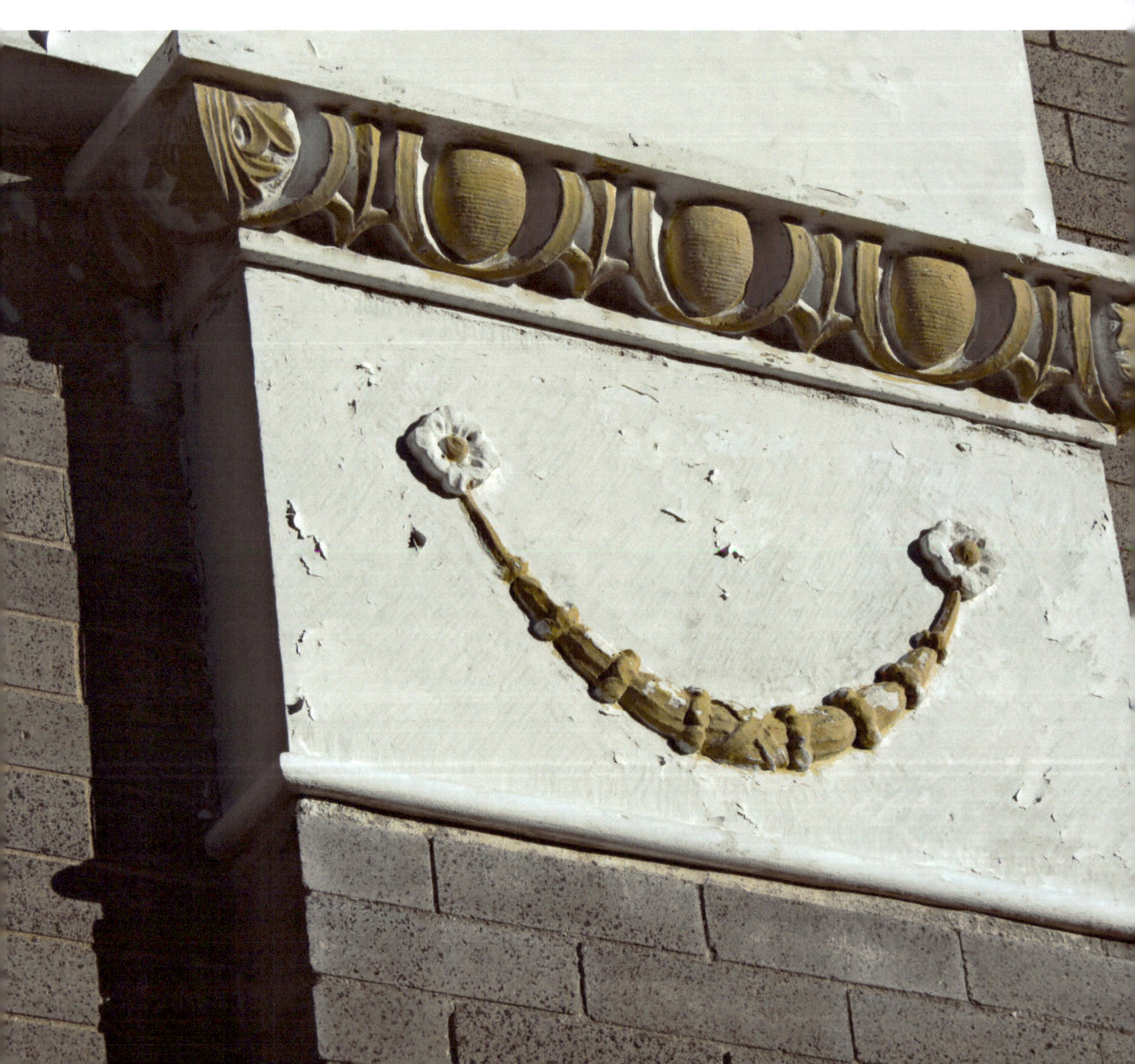

Across from the Pawn Shop.

These last few, see if you can find them on your own, without a hint!

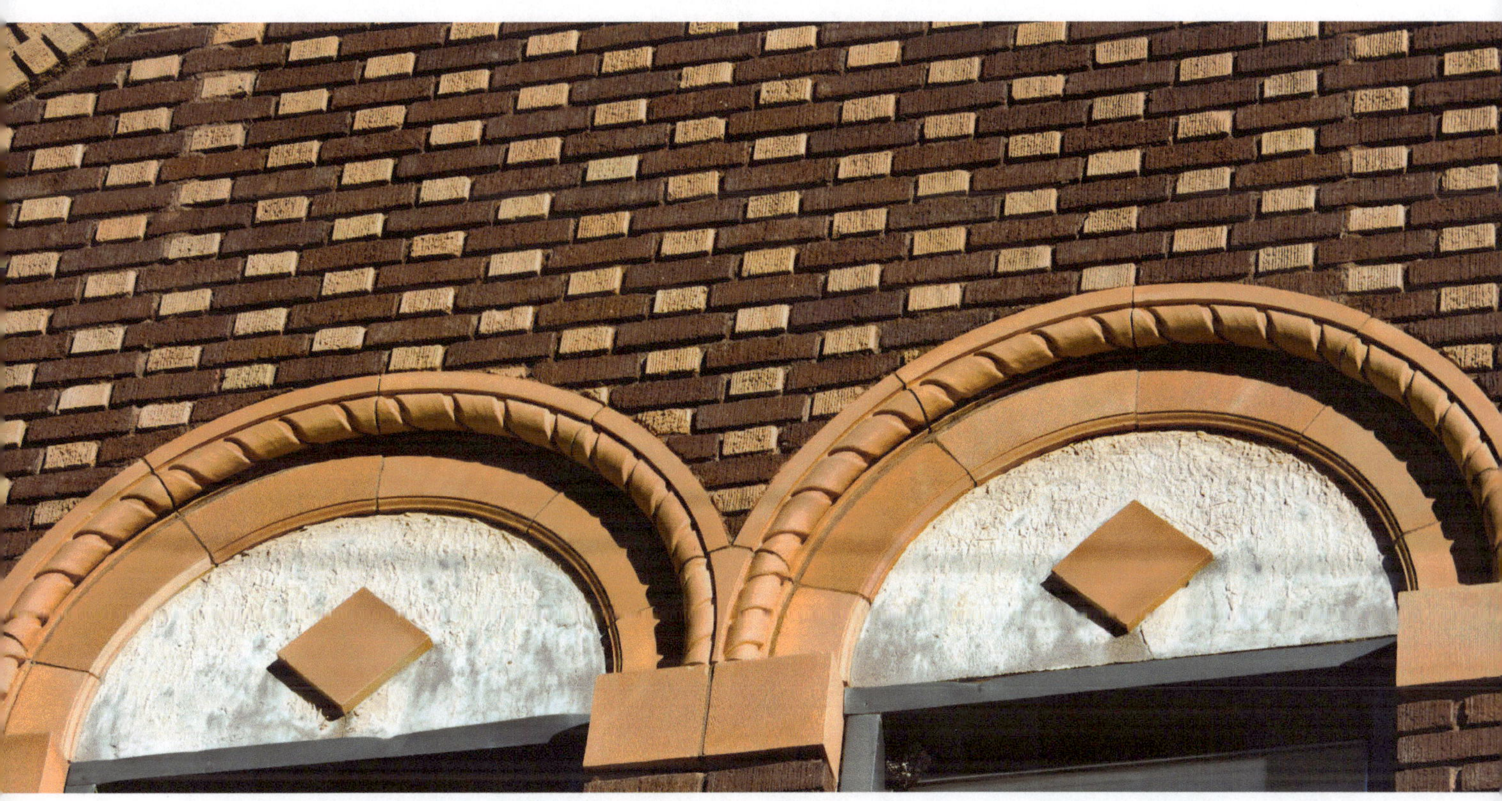

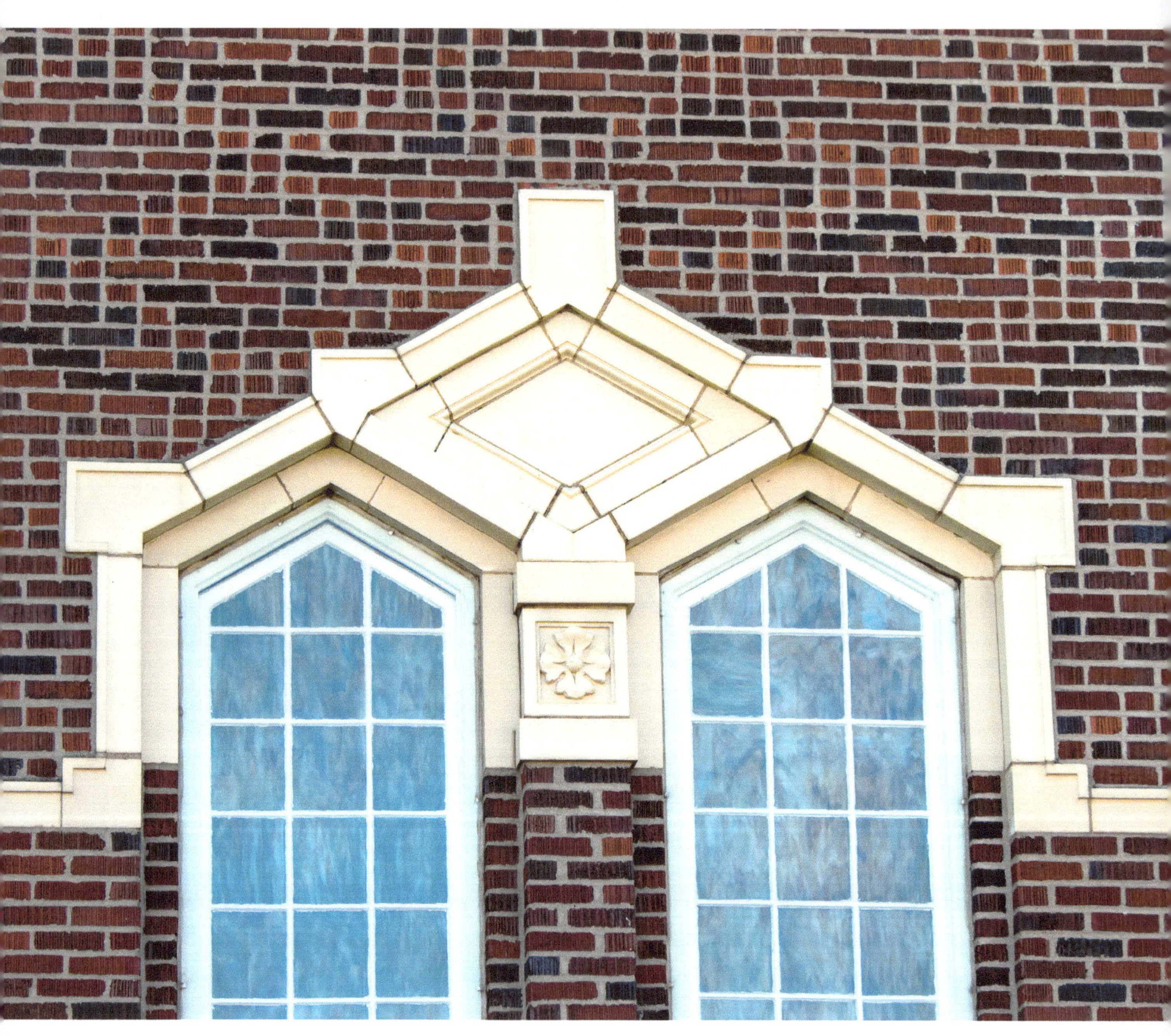
It is in the downtown area.

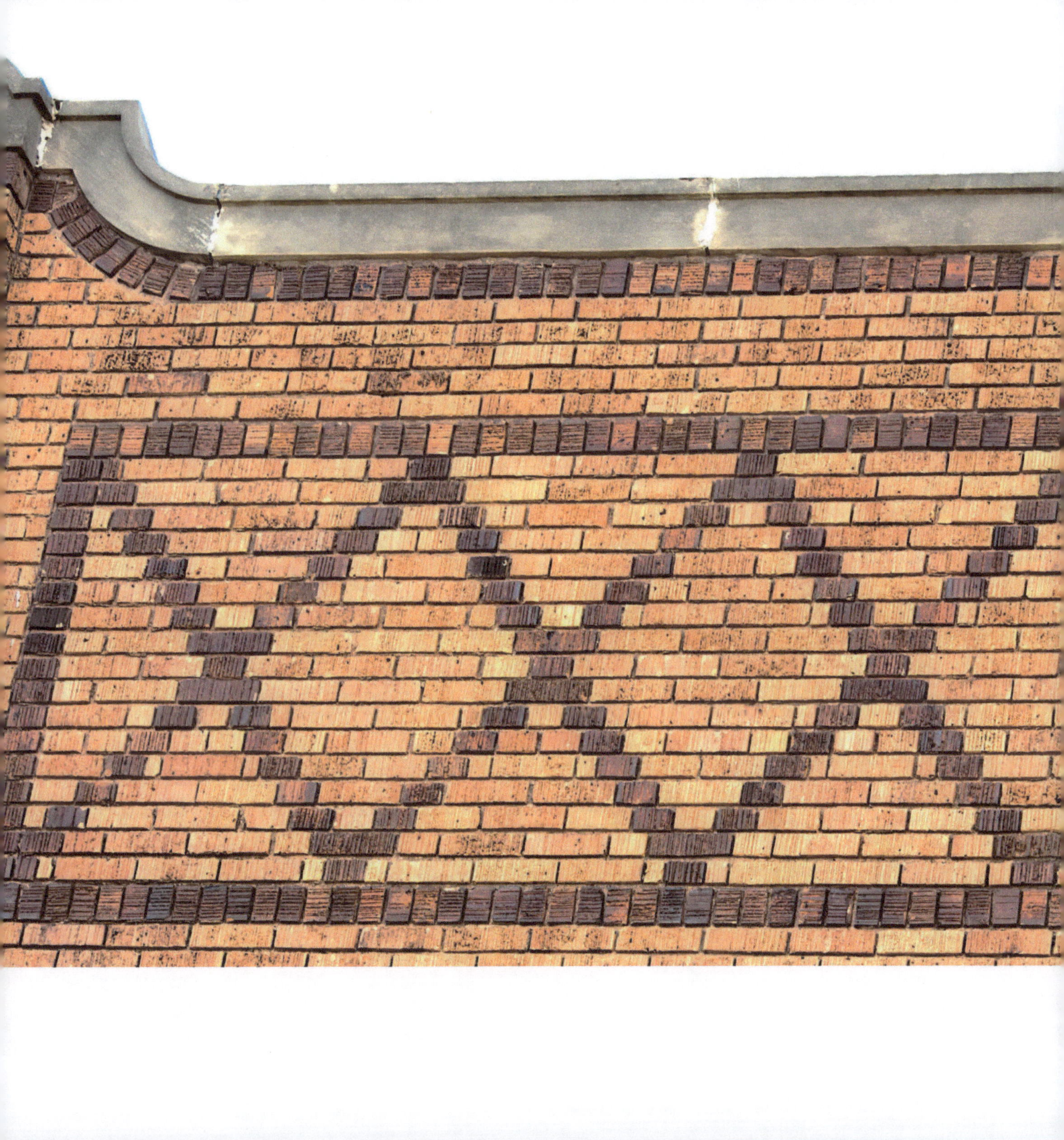

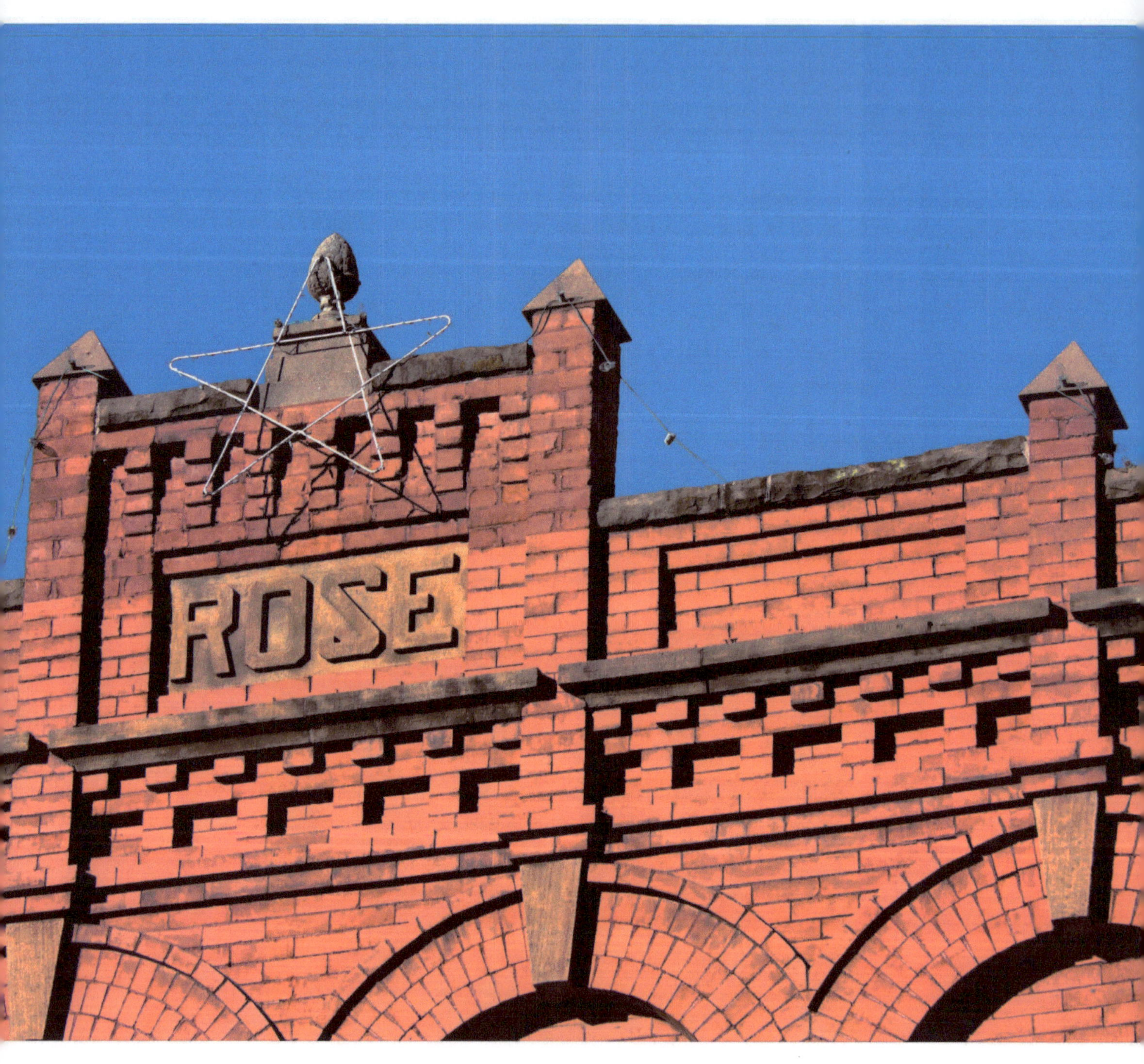

ROSE

We hope you enjoyed your Okmulgee Adventure! Thanks for playing along!

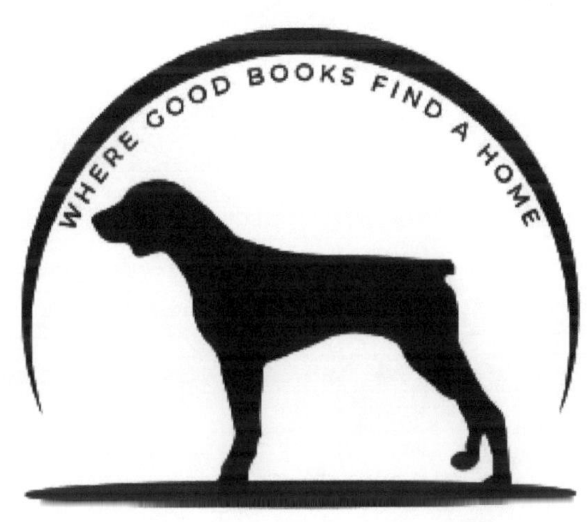

All photography by Dale Fillmore
Copyright 2023
Published by Fine Dog Press, Okmulgee County, Oklahoma

www.ingramcontent.com/pod-product-compliance
Lightning Source LLC
Chambersburg PA
CBHW042125030726
47599CB00002B/352